Hal Leonard Student Piano Library

Piano Lessons

Book 4

Authors
Barbara Kreader, Fred Kern, Phillip Keveren

Consultants
Mona Rejino, Tony Caramia,
Bruce Berr, Richard Rejino

Director,
Educational Keyboard Publications
Margaret Otwell

Editor
Carol Klose

Illustrator
Fred Bell

To access audio visit:
www.halleonard.com/mylibrary
Enter code:

7821-1438-3126-7476

FOREWORD

When music excites our interest and imagination, we eagerly put our hearts into learning it. The music in the **Hal Leonard Student Piano Library** encourages practise, progress, confidence, and best of all – success! Over 1,000 students and teachers in a nationwide test market responded with enthusiasm to the:

- variety of styles and moods
- natural rhythmic flow, singable melodies and lyrics
- "best ever" teacher accompaniments
- improvisations integrated throughout the **Lesson Books**
- orchestrated accompaniments included in audio and MIDI formats.

When new concepts have an immediate application to the music, the effort it takes to learn these skills seems worth it. Test market teachers and students were especially excited about the:

- "realistic" pacing that challenges without overwhelming
- clear and concise presentation of concepts that allows room for a teacher's individual approach
- uncluttered page layout that keeps the focus on the music.

The **Piano Practice Games** books are preparation activities to coordinate technique, concepts, and creativity with the actual music in **Piano Lessons**. In addition, the **Piano Theory Workbook** presents fun writing activities for review, and the **Piano Solos** series reinforces concepts with challenging performance repertoire.

The **Hal Leonard Student Piano Library** is the result of the efforts of many individuals. We extend our gratitude to all the teachers, students and colleagues who shared their energy and creative input. May this method guide your learning as you bring this music to life.

Best wishes,

Book: ISBN 978-0-7935-8621-6
Book/Audio: ISBN 978-0-634-08426-7

HAL•LEONARD®
CORPORATION
7777 W. BLUEMOUND RD. P.O. BOX 13819 MILWAUKEE, WI 53213

Copyright © 1998 by HAL LEONARD CORPORATION
International Copyright Secured   All Rights Reserved

For all works contained herein:
Unauthorized copying, arranging, adapting, recording, Internet posting, public performance,
or other distribution of the printed or recorded music in this publication is an infringement of copyright.
Infringers are liable under the law.

Visit Hal Leonard Online at
www.halleonard.com

REVIEW OF BOOK THREE

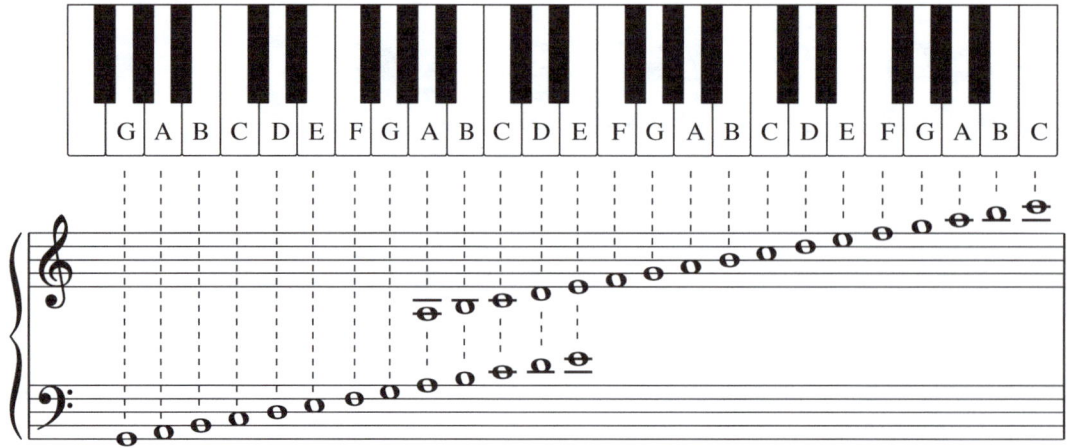

NOTE VALUES

quaver notes
two quaver notes fill the
time of one crotchet note

dotted-crotchet quaver pattern
fills the time of two crotchet notes

INTERVALS

Interval of a 6th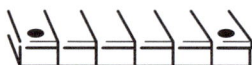

semitone
the distance from one key to
another, with no key in between

tone
the distance from one key to
another, with one key in between

FIVE-FINGER PATTERNS

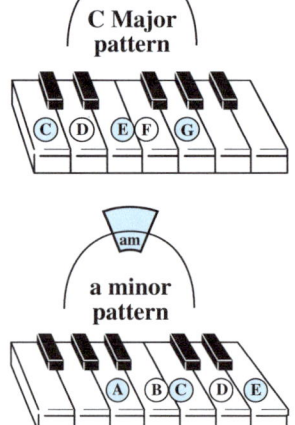
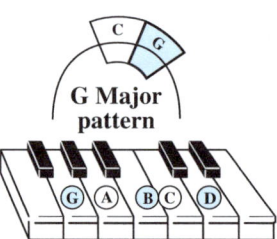
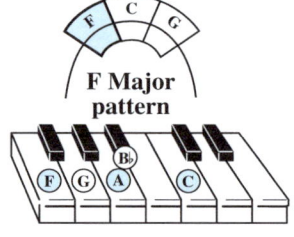
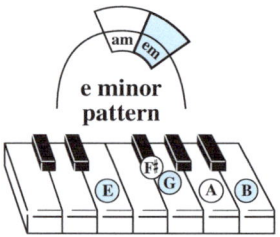
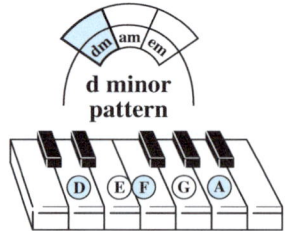

MUSICAL TERMS

time signature 2/4   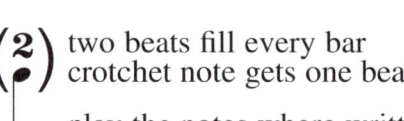 two beats fill every bar
crotchet note gets one beat

loco   play the notes where written

a tempo   return to the original tempo

D.S. (Dal Segno) al Fine   return to 𝄋 (*segno*) and play to the end (*fine*)

D.C. (Da Capo) al Coda   return to the beginning and play to the first
coda sign ⊕; then skip to the next coda sign ⊕

15ma   play two octaves higher than written

CONTENTS

UNIT 1 RELATED FIVE-FINGER PATTERNS
*✓

___ My Own Song .... *C Major & A Minor improvisation* 4
___ Rustic Dance .... *crossing 2 over 1* 5
___ Carpet Ride 6
___ My Own Song .... *G Major & E Minor improvisation* 7
___ Mister Banjo .... 𝄾 8
___ Morning Bells .... *syncopated pedalling* 9
___ Ribbons *7ths* 10

PLAYING IN C MAJOR & A MINOR

UNIT 2 EXPLORING THE SCALES

___ Scale Preparation .... *sliding 3 under 1* 11
___ Moving On Up .... *C Major scale* 12
___ Calypso Cat .... *key signature* 13
___ Jig 3/8 6/8 14
___ Two-Four-Six-Eight 16
___ Relative Scales 18
___ Moving On Up .... *A Minor scale* 19
___ Allegro 20
___ Etude 21

UNIT 3 DISCOVERING THE PRIMARY TRIADS

___ Take It Easy .... *C Major root position triads* 22
___ Close By .... *C Major close position triads & improvisation* 23
___ Jumping Beans .... *octave* 24
___ Relay Race .... *common time* 𝄴 25
___ A Minor Tango .... *A Minor triads & improvisation* 26
___ All The Pretty Little Horses 27
___ Joshua Fit The Battle Of Jericho .... *theme & variations, changing metres* 28

PLAYING IN G MAJOR & E MINOR

UNIT 4 EXPLORING THE SCALES

___ Moving On Up .... *G Major scale* 30
___ Spanish Dance 31
___ True Blues .... *cut common time* 𝄵 32
___ Blues For A Count .... *triplets* 34
___ Doo Wop Ditty 35
___ Moving On Up .... *E Minor scale* 36
___ Wandering 37

UNIT 5 DISCOVERING THE PRIMARY TRIADS

___ Ready To Rock! .... *G Major triads* 38
___ The Bass Singer 39
___ On The Prowl .... *E Minor triads & improvisation* 40
___ Starry Night .... *finger substitution* 41
___ Rhapsody .... *tenuto* 42
___ Longing 44
___ Presto 45
___ Allegro from *Eine Kleine Nachtmusik* 46
___ Audio Track List 48

Students can check pieces as they play them.

UNIT 1

Related Five-Finger Patterns

Every major five-finger pattern has a related minor five-finger pattern.

To find the related minor pattern:
1. Play the major pattern with your L.H.
2. Place your R.H. thumb one tone above the highest note of the major pattern.
3. Play the minor pattern with your R.H.

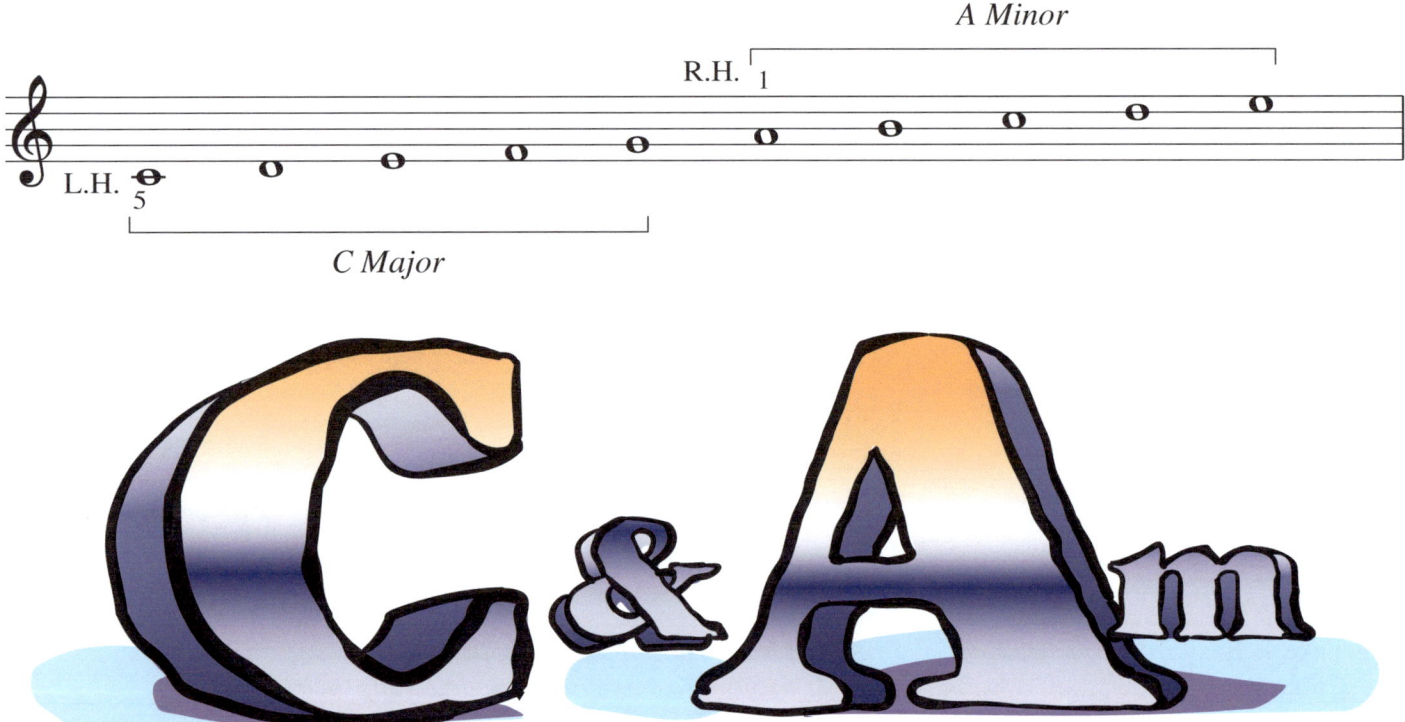

My Own Song
in C Major & A Minor

As you listen to the accompaniment, improvise a melody using the **C Major** pattern with your L.H. and the **A Minor** pattern (relative minor) with your R.H. Begin playing in the C Major pattern. Your teacher will tell you when to change to the A Minor pattern.

Accompaniment (Student improvises one octave higher than shown above.)

Rustic Dance

Barbara Kreader

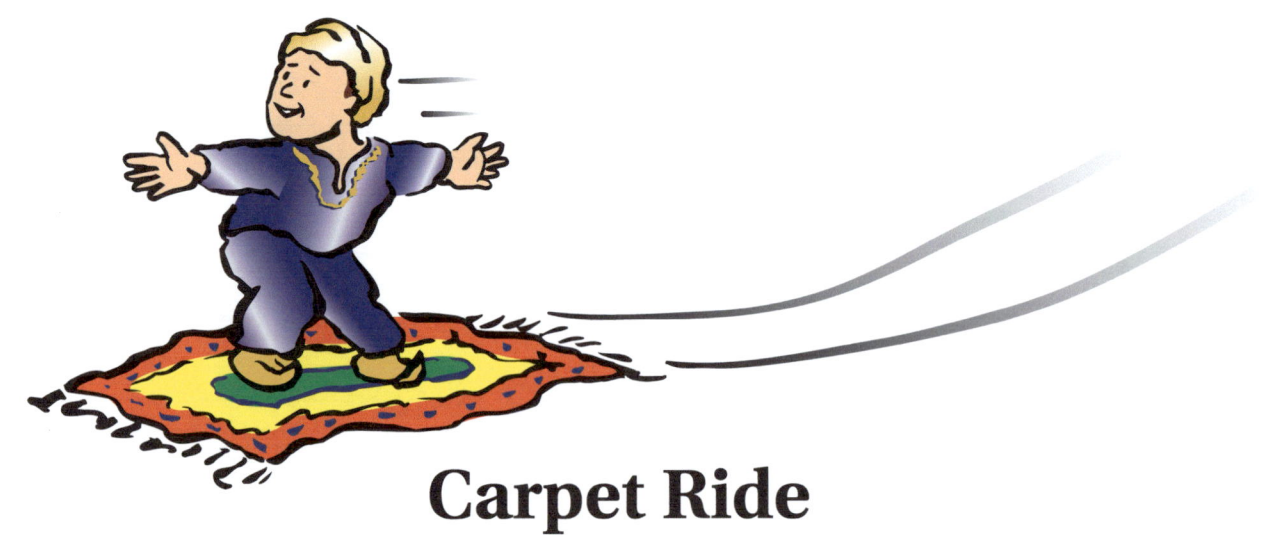

Carpet Ride

Mysteriously (♩=135)

Phillip Keveren

Cross 2 over 1

My Own Song
in G Major & E Minor

As you listen to the accompaniment, improvise a melody using the **G Major** pattern with your L.H. and the **E Minor** pattern (relative minor) with your R.H. Begin playing in the G Major pattern. Your teacher will tell you when to change to the E Minor pattern.

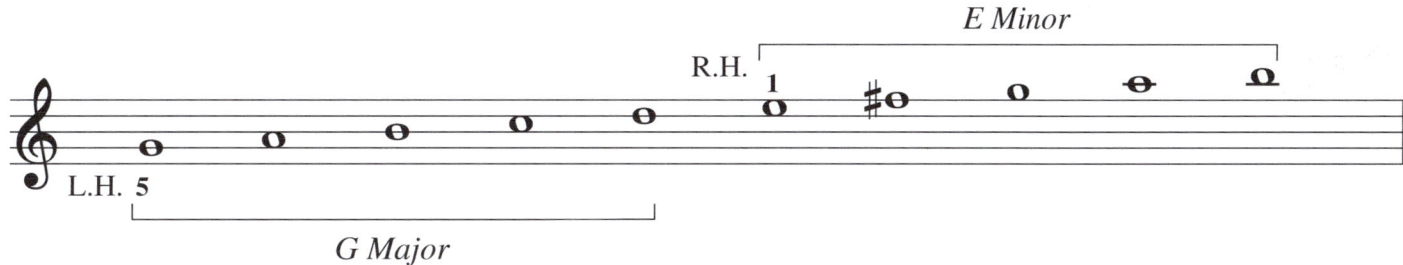

Accompaniment (Student improvises one octave higher than shown above.)

QUAVER REST

A **Quaver Rest** fills the time of one quaver note.

SYNCOPATION

Music becomes **syncopated** when the rhythmic emphasis shifts to a weak beat – either ahead of or behind the strong beats in the bar.

Clap and count these patterns:

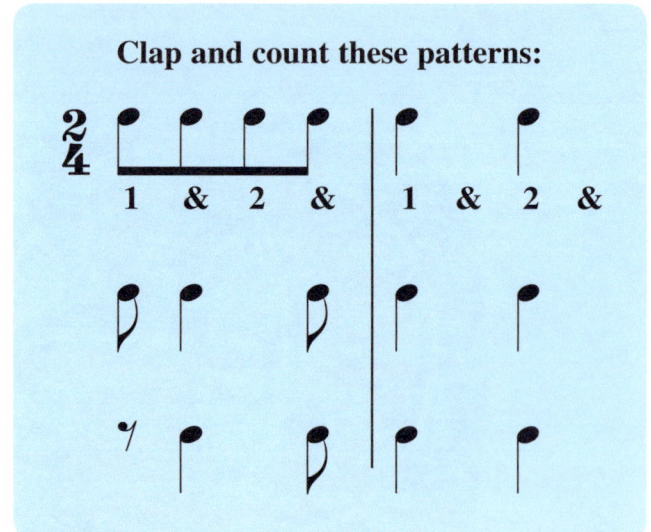

Mister Banjo

Creole
Arranged by Phillip Keveren

Spirited (♩=170)

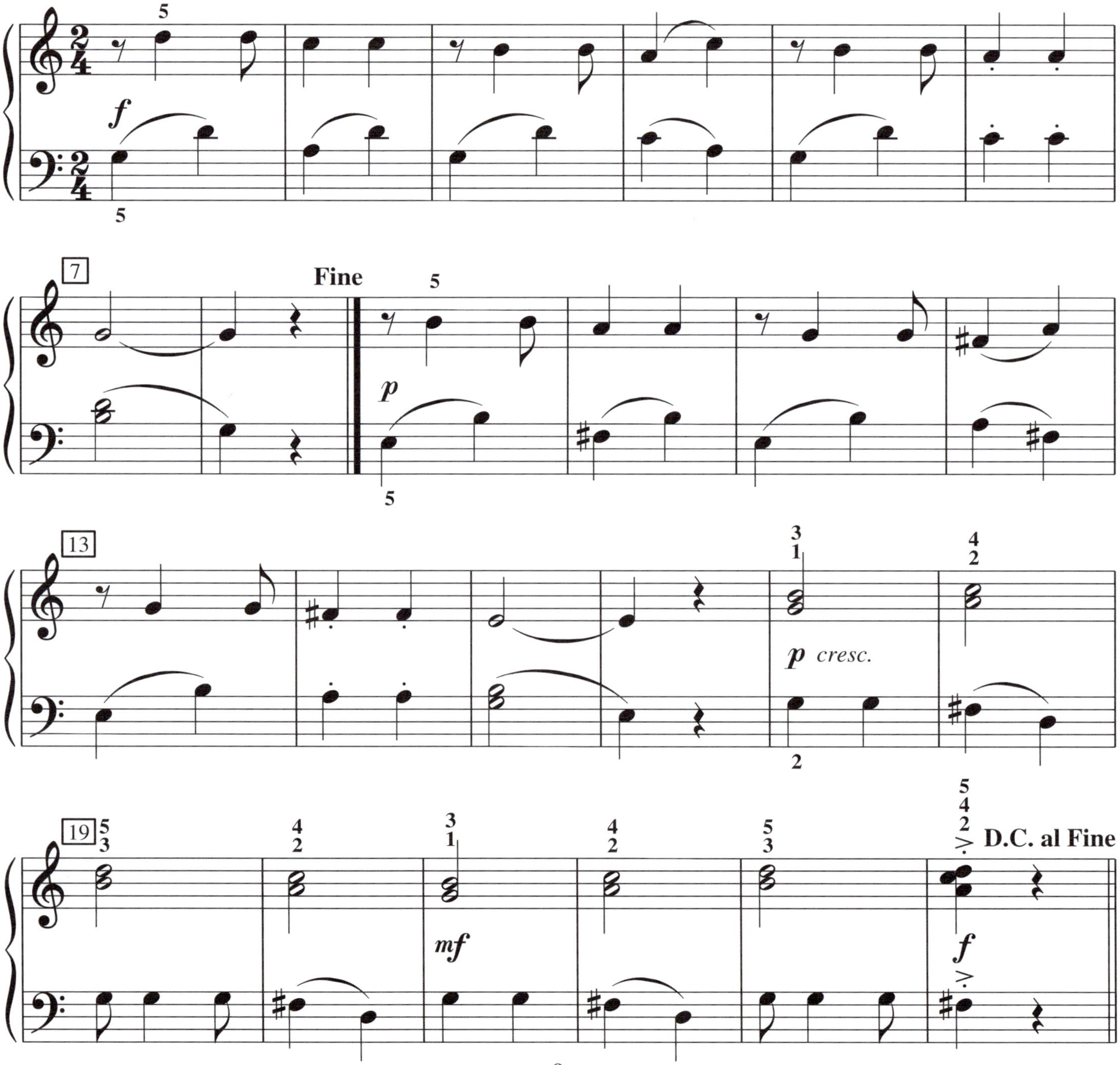

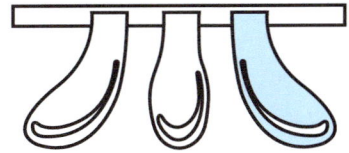

SYNCOPATED PEDALLING

When you press the sustain pedal, the notes will continue to ring after you release the keys. To produce a smooth sound, release and press the pedal quickly. Always keep your heel on the floor.

Change the sustain pedal **immediately after** playing the notes. Pedalling too late will cause the sound to blur; pedalling too early will cause a break in the sound.

Morning Bells

With energy (♩=135)

Phillip Keveren

INTERVAL of a 7th

On the piano, a 7th
- skips five keys
- skips five letters

On the staff, a 7th skips from either line to line or space to space and skips five letter names.

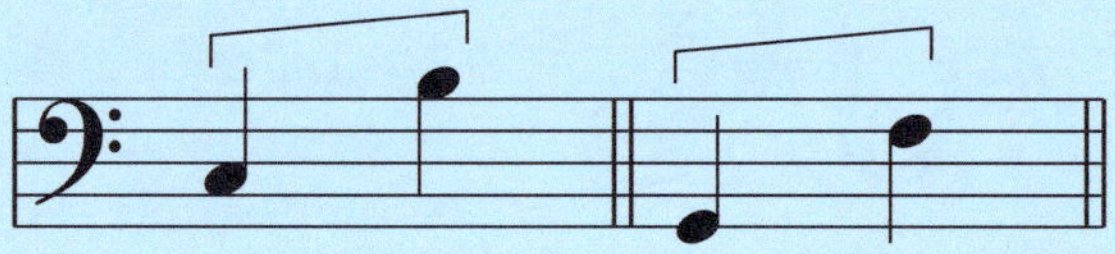

Ribbons

Smoothly (♩=95)

Fred Kern

Second time both hands 8va

a tempo on repeat

To Coda

D.C. al Coda

rit.

CODA *loco*

Cross 2 over 1

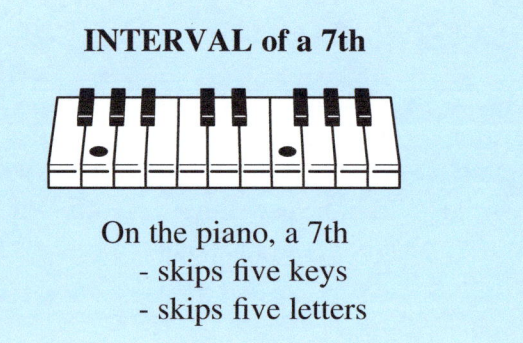

10

UNIT 2

MAJOR SCALE PATTERNS

All **Major Scale Patterns** are made up of eight notes in the following order of semitones and tones.

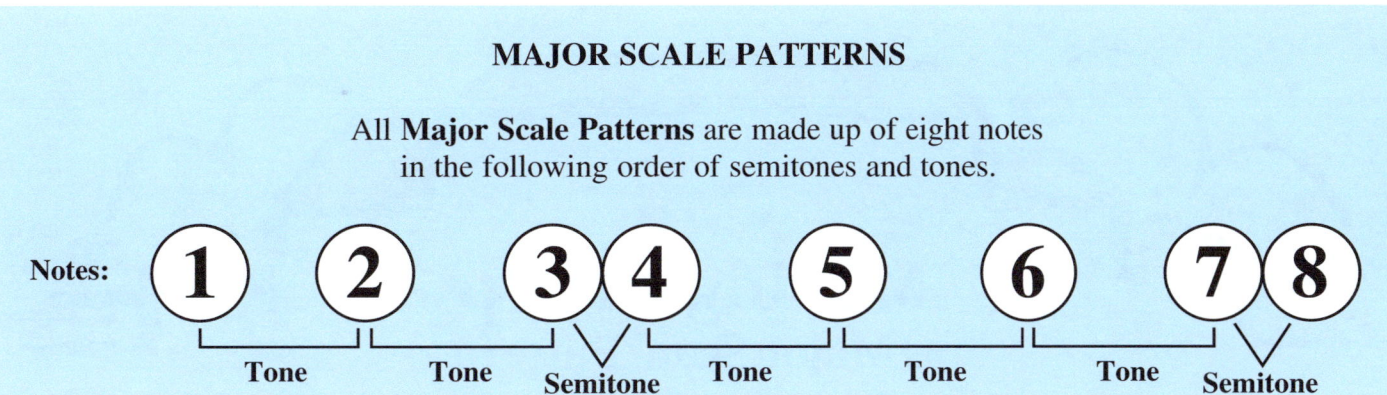

C Major Scale

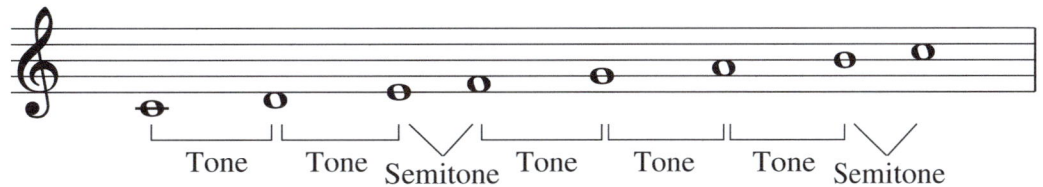

Scale Preparation

Prepare to play a scale by first practising the thumb movements.
Let your arm guide your fingers smoothly up and down the keyboard.

*Allegretto

Katherine Glaser

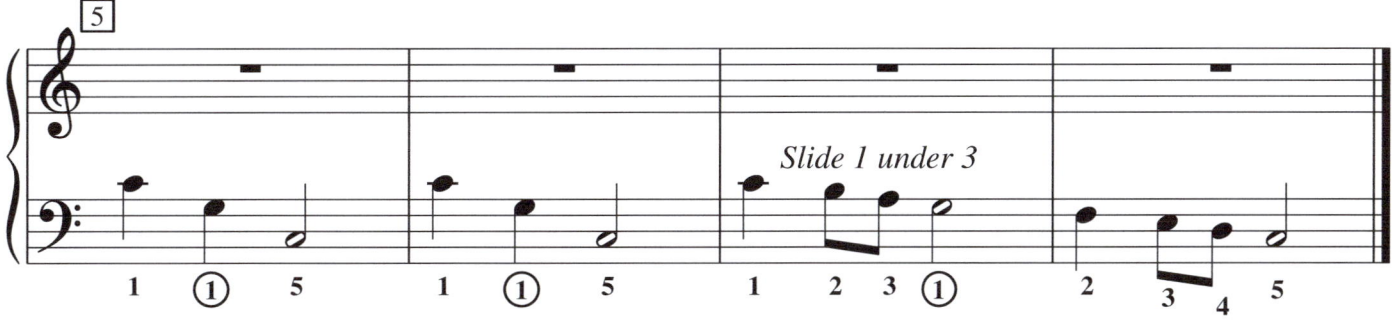

Accompaniment (Student plays one octave higher.)

* quickly, but not as fast as Allegro

Moving On Up
C Major Scale Pattern

*Moderato

mf

Cross 3 over 1 **Slide 1 under 3**

Slide 1 under 3 **Cross 3 over 1**

Accompaniment (Student plays two octaves higher than written.)

Moderato (♩=110)

mp

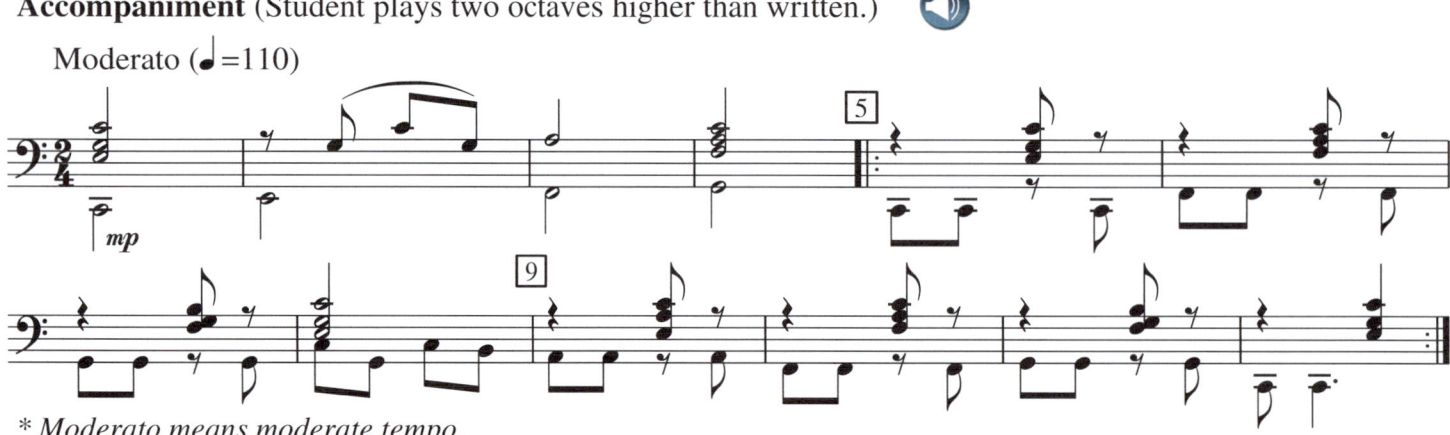

Moderato means moderate tempo.

KEY SIGNATURE

Every piece opens with a **key signature**. It identifies the scale pattern the composer used and tells you which notes to play sharp or flat throughout the piece.

Clap and count:

Calypso Cat

Key of C Major
Key signature: *no sharps, no flats*

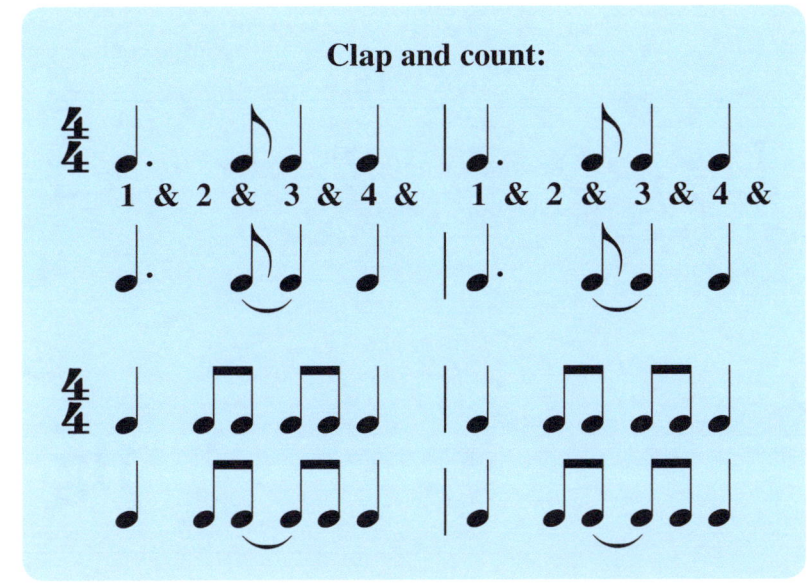

Happily (♩=140)

Phillip Keveren

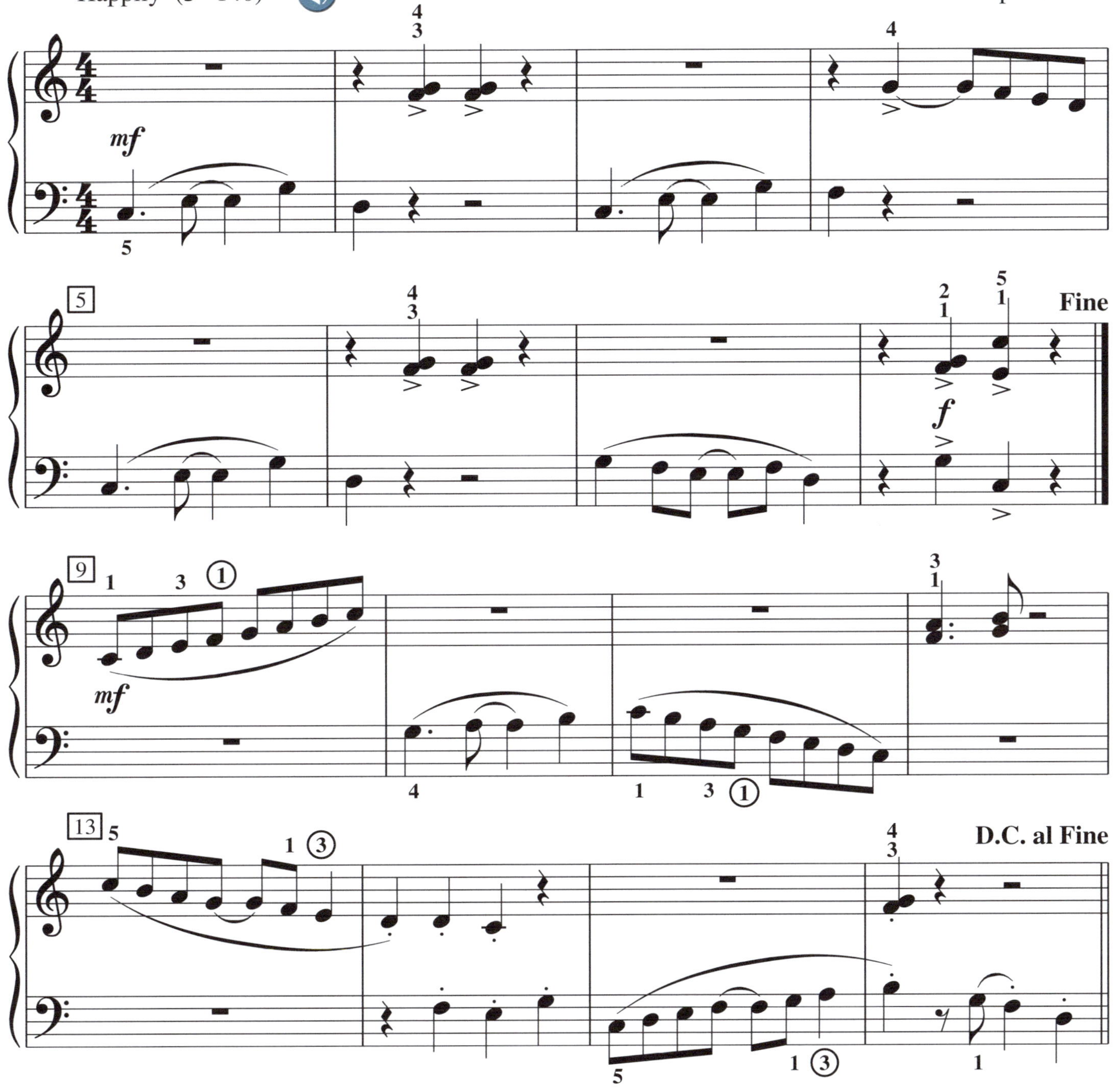

3/8 TIME SIGNATURE

3/8 (3/♪) = three quaver notes fill one bar
= quaver note gets one beat

Clap and count:

Jig

Irish
Arranged by Fred Kern

Lively (♩. =86)

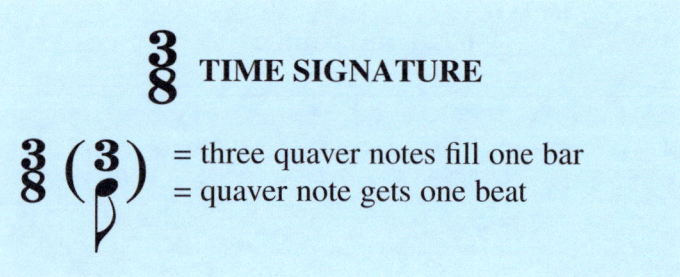

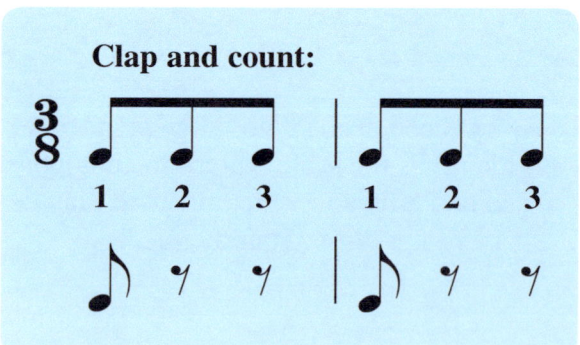

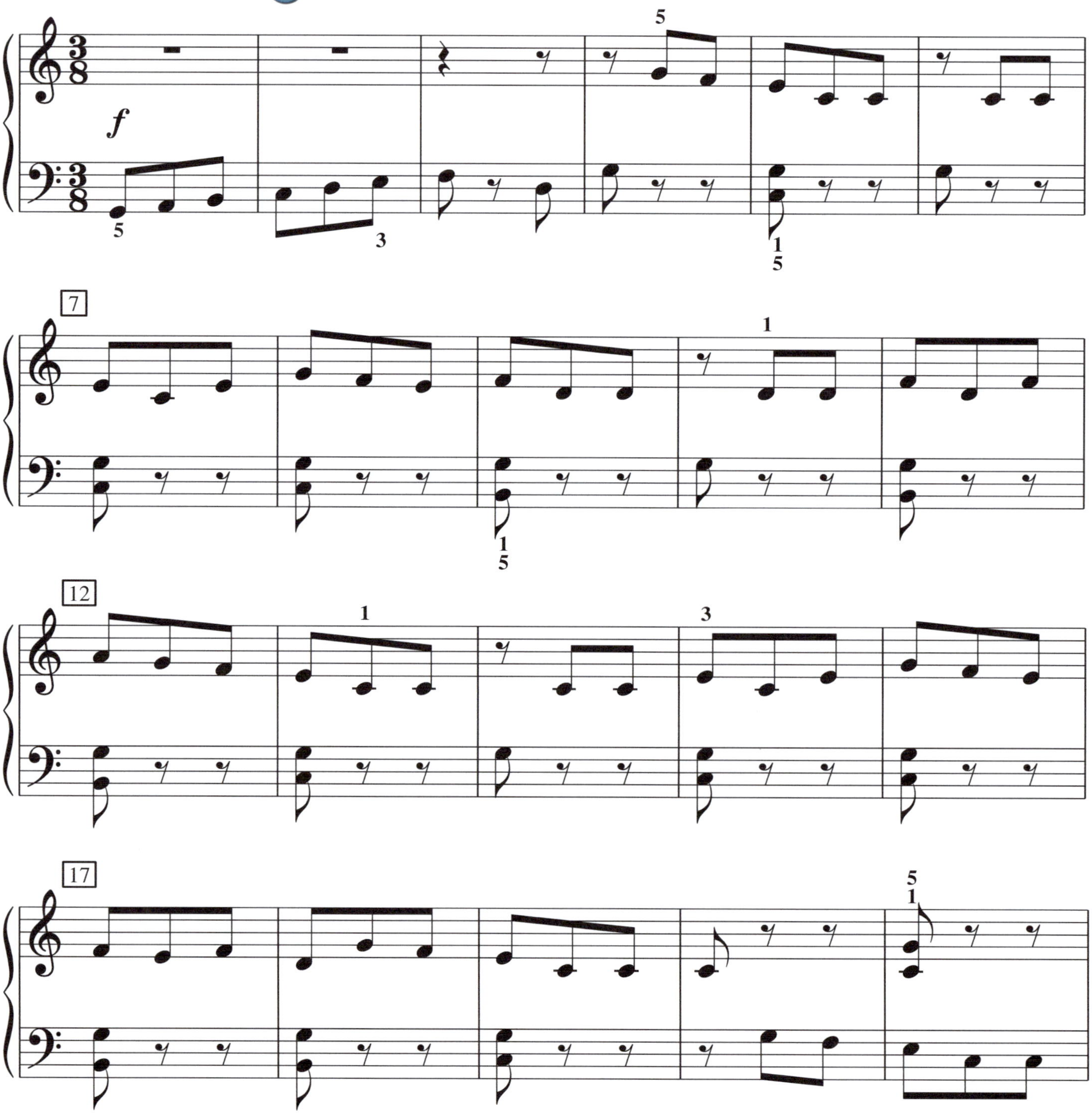

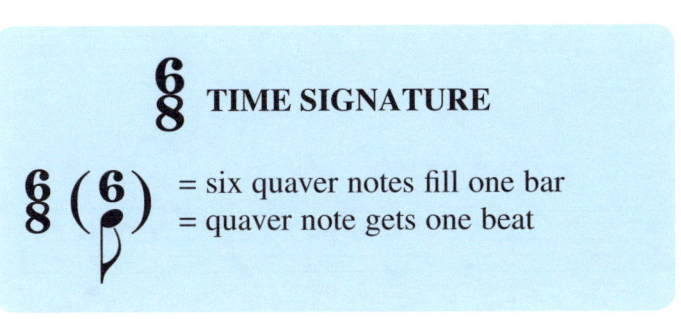

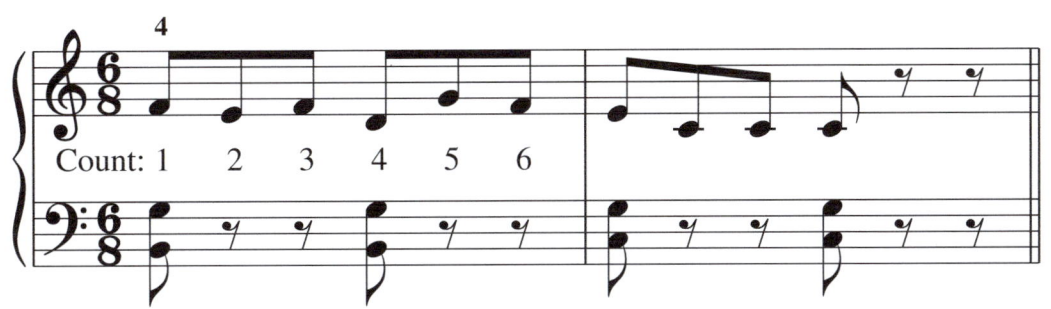

ACCIDENTALS

Sharps (♯), Flats (♭) or Naturals (♮) added to a piece outside the key signature are called **Accidentals**.

Two-Four-Six-Eight

Relative Scales

Every Major Scale has a Relative Minor. It begins on the sixth note of the major scale.

A is the sixth note of the C Major scale. C Major and A Minor are **Relative Scales** because they have the same **Key Signature:** *no sharps and no flats.*

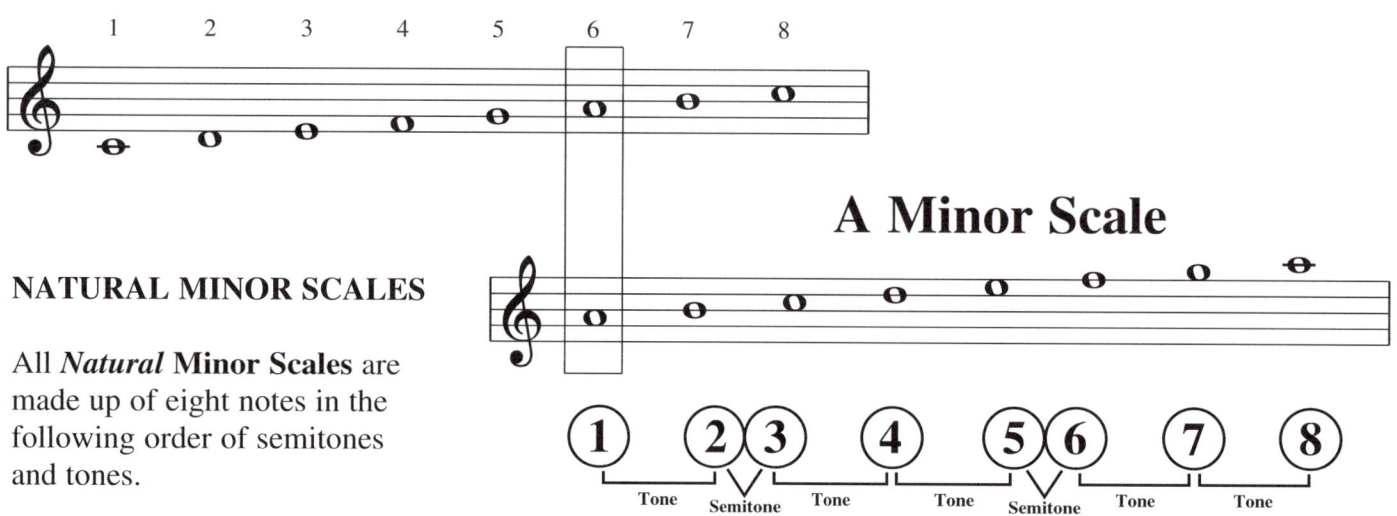

NATURAL MINOR SCALES

All *Natural* Minor Scales are made up of eight notes in the following order of semitones and tones.

HARMONIC MINOR SCALES

The *Harmonic* form of the minor scale raises the seventh note one semitone indicated by an accidental. The A Harmonic Minor Scale has a G♯.

For a quick way to find the relative minor, *move down 3 semitones* from the first note of the major scale.

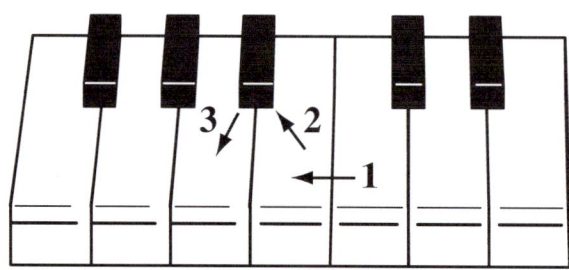

"A" is 3 semitones below "C".

Moving On Up
A Minor Scale Patterns

First, play the *Natural Minor Scale* with no sharps.
On the repeat, play the *Harmonic Minor Scale* with the raised 7th (G#).

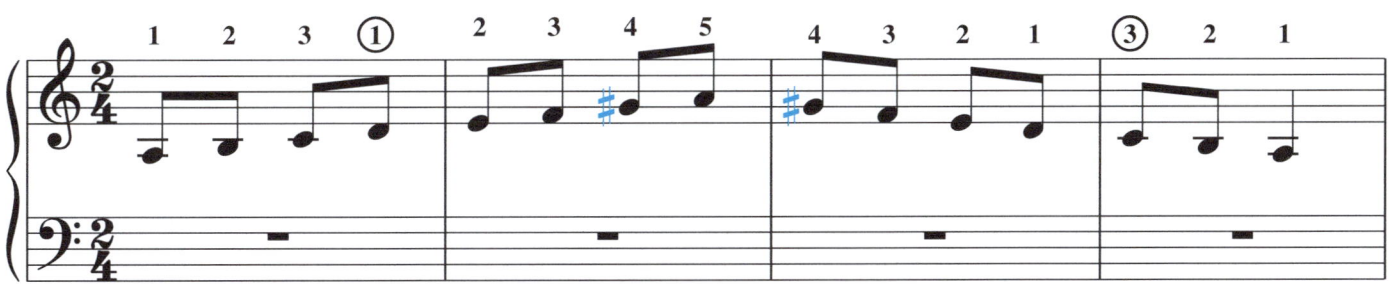

Accompaniment (Student plays two octaves higher than written.)

First, play the natural form with no sharps or flats.
On the repeat, play the harmonic form with the raised 7th (G#).

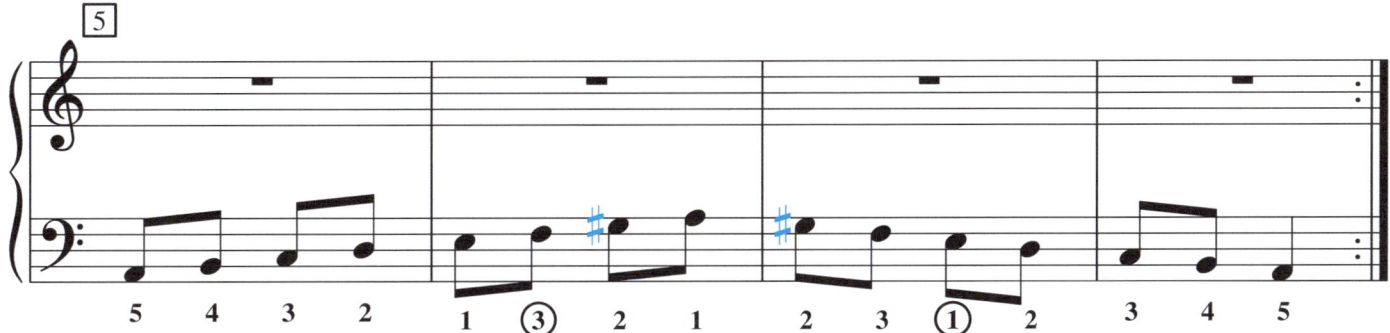

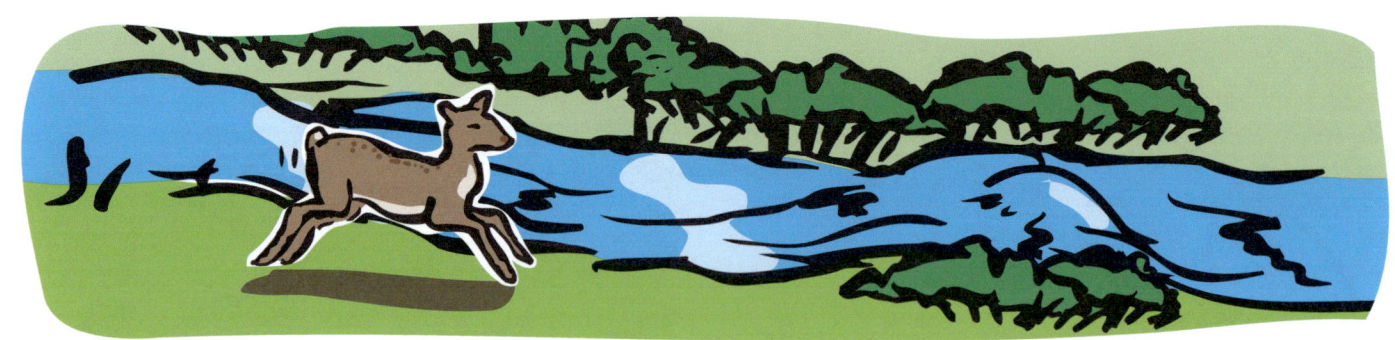

Allegro

Key of A Minor
Key signature: ____________

Cornelius Gurlitt
(1820-1901)
Op. 82, No. 52

Allegro (♩=170)

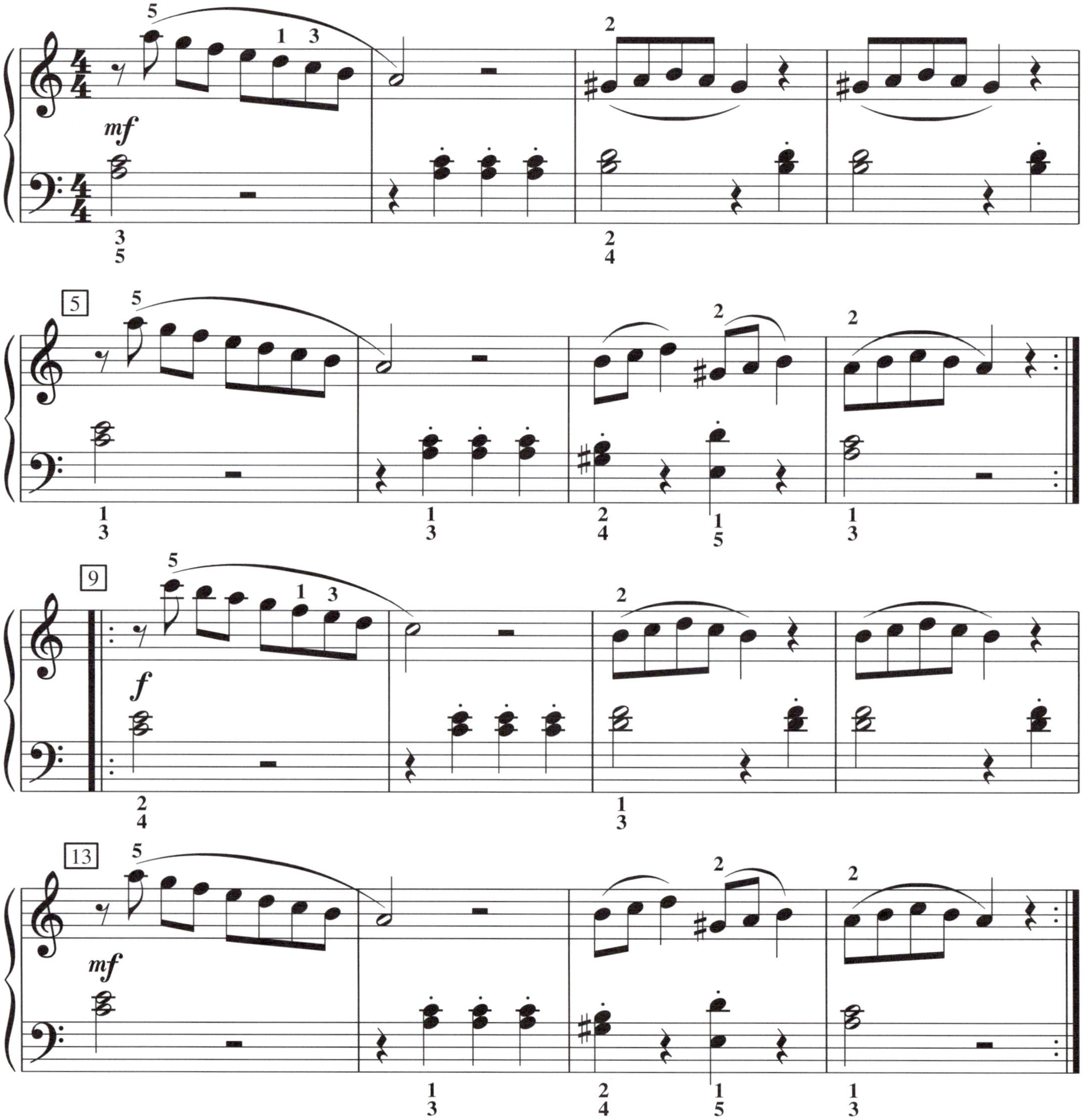

*Etude

Key of A Minor

Key signature: _____

Ludwig Schytte
(1848-1909)

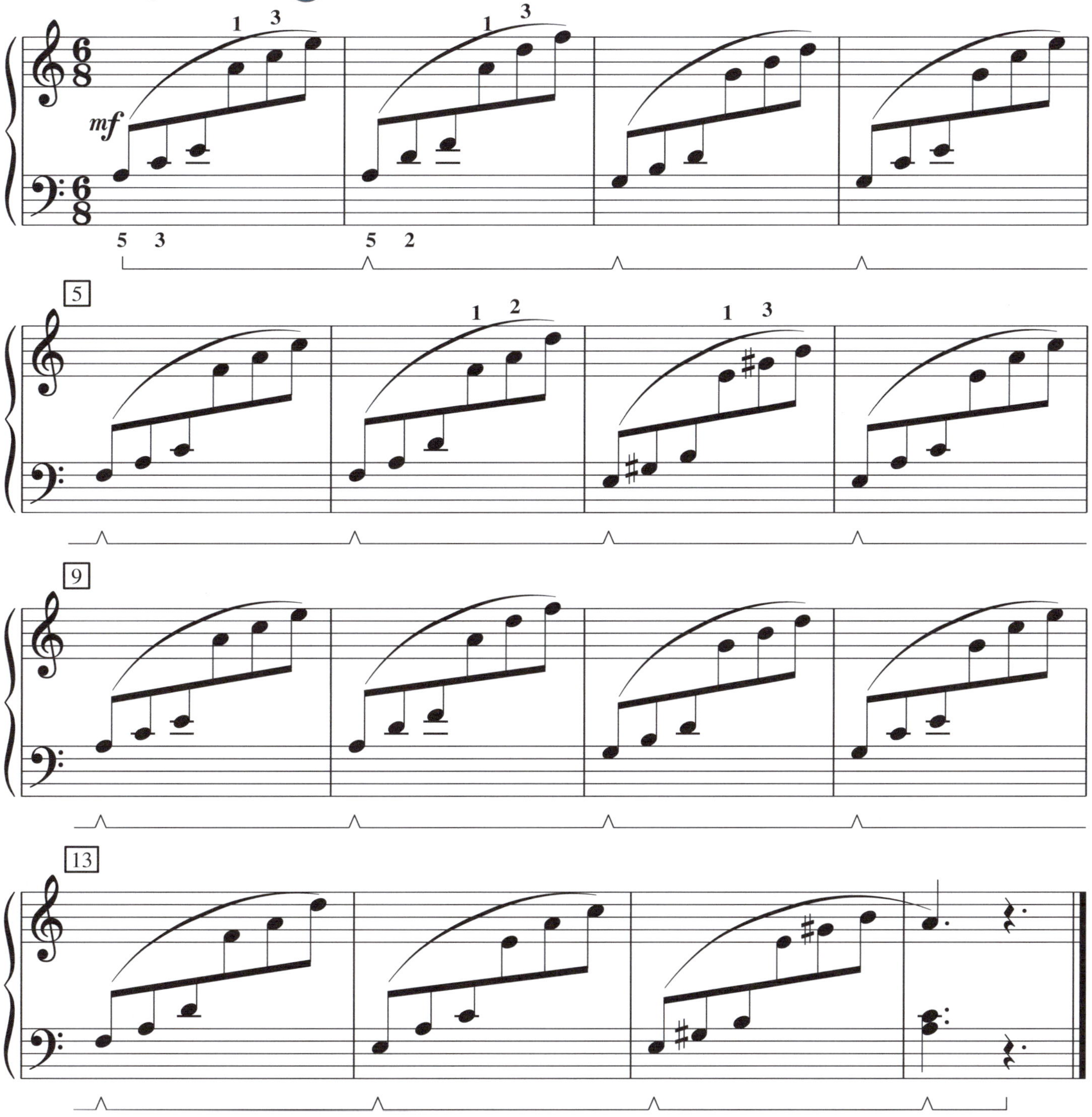

Flowing (♩.=87)

*Etude means a study or exercise piece.

UNIT 3

TRIADS IN ROOT POSITION

Root Position Triads can be built on any note of the scale and are written on three lines or three spaces.

PRIMARY TRIADS

Chords built on the 1st, 4th and 5th notes of the scale are called **Primary Triads: Tonic (I), Sub-dominant (IV), Dominant (V).**

The Primary Triads in C Major are:

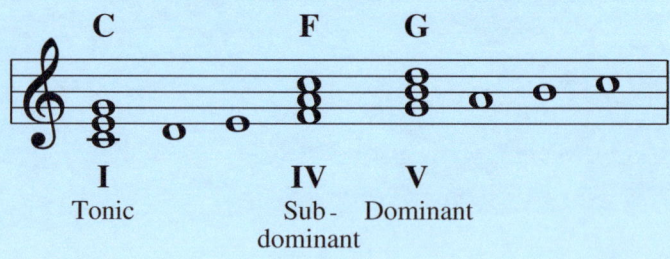

Take It Easy

Chord warm-up in root position

Relaxed

Phillip Keveren

Teacher Solo (Play one octave higher than written.)

Relaxed (♩=130)

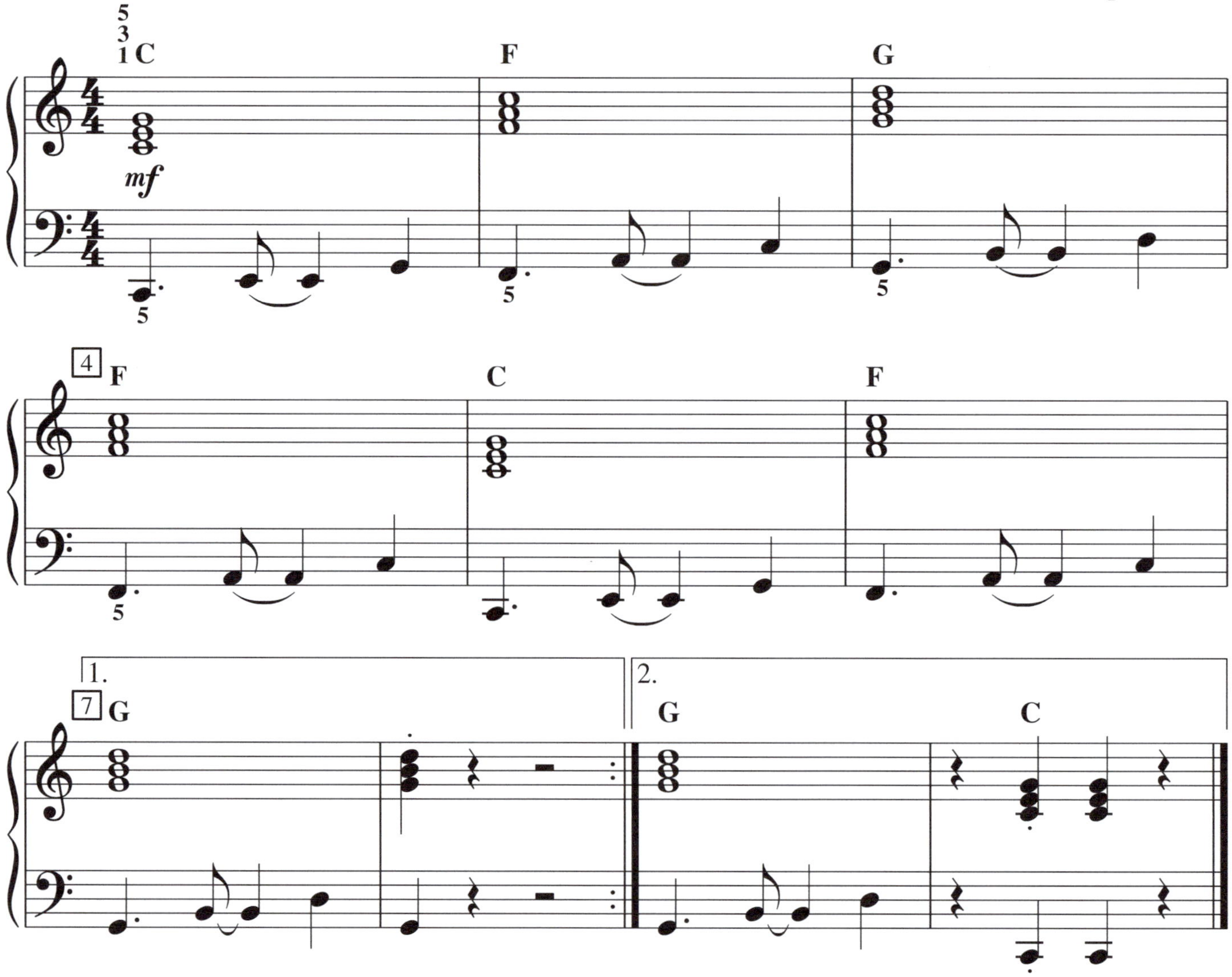

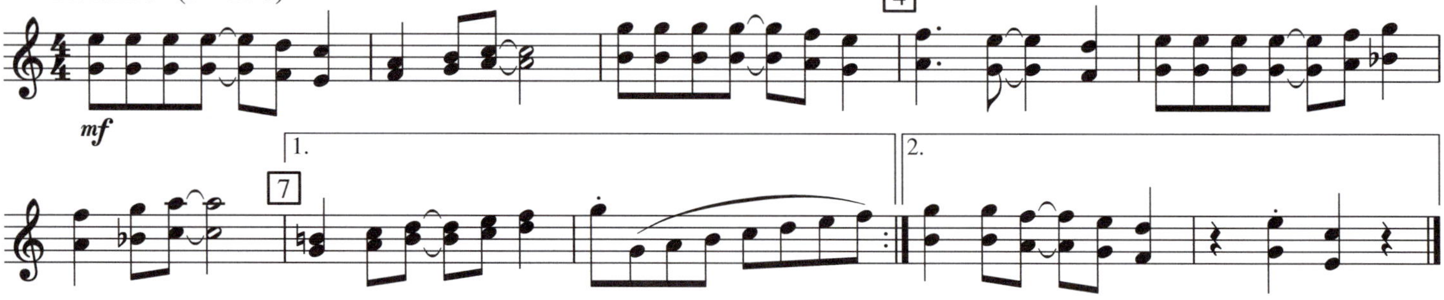

PRIMARY TRIADS IN CLOSE POSITION

The notes in root position triads can be rearranged (inverted) to create closer movement from one chord to the next.

The **G7 chord** includes F, the 7th note above G.

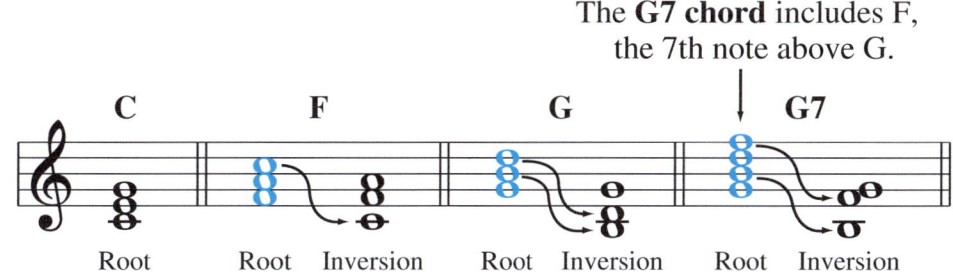

Close By

Chord warm-up in close position

Flowing

Phillip Keveren

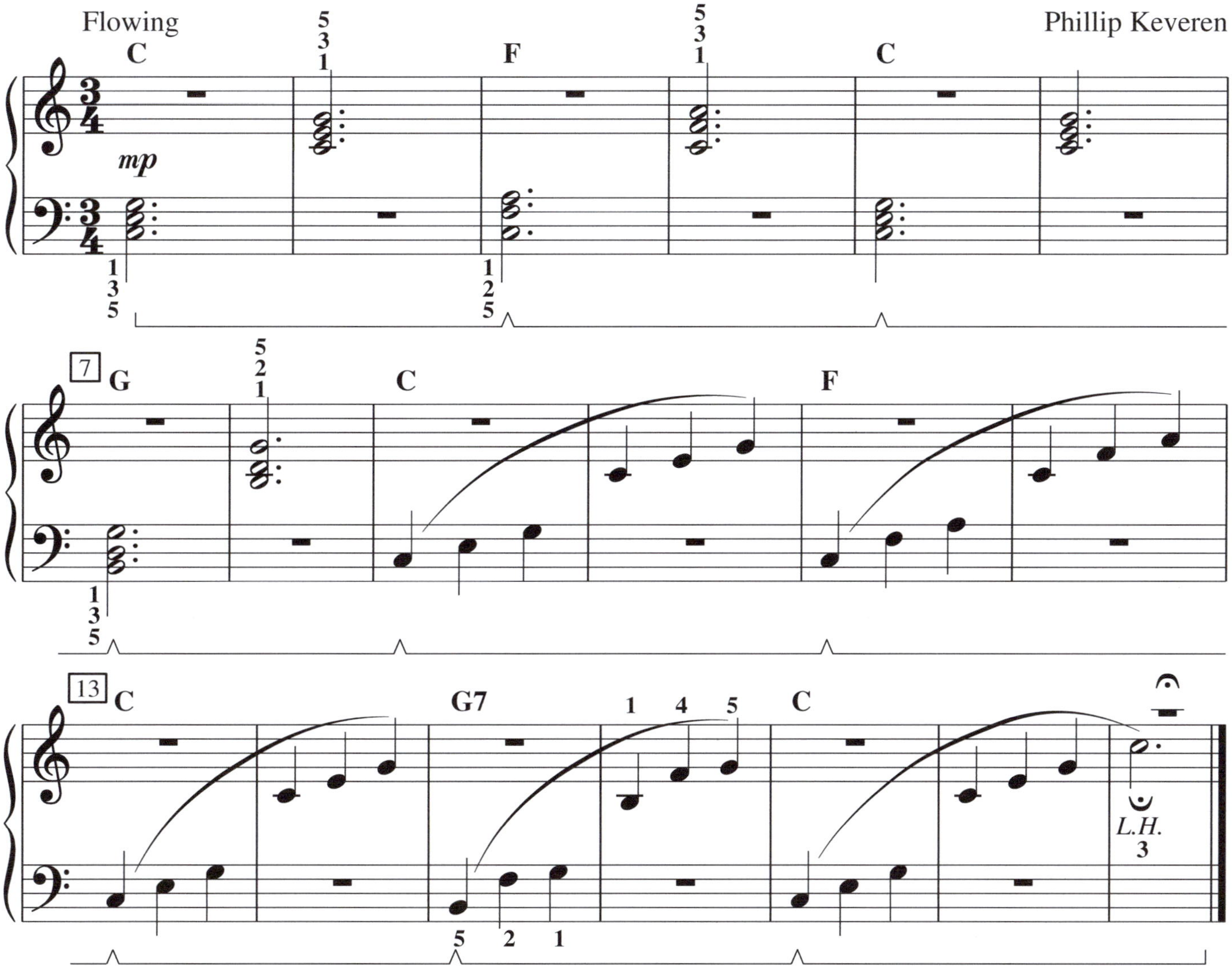

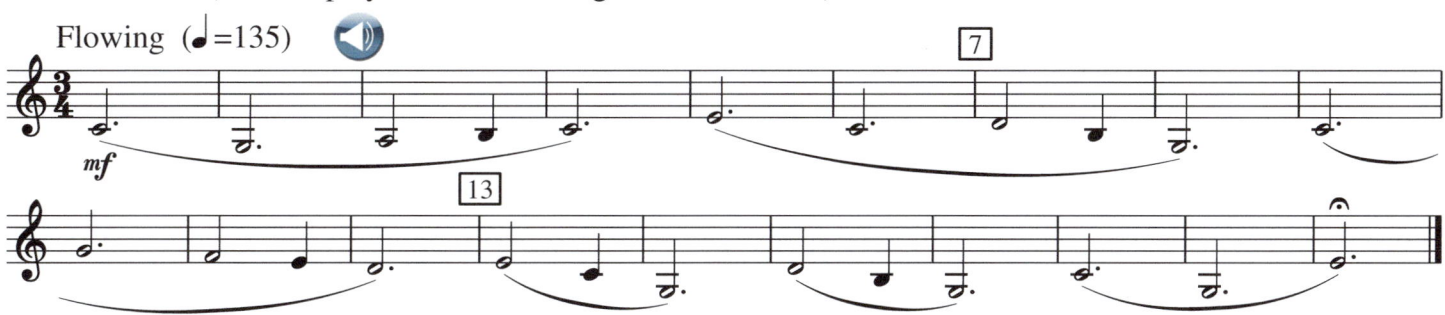

Teacher Solo (Student plays two octaves higher than written.)

Flowing (♩=135)

My Own Song

Improvisation using *C Major Triads*

As your teacher plays the student part to *Close By,* improvise a new melody in the key of **C Major**.

INTERVAL of an OCTAVE (8th)

On the piano, an octave
- skips six keys
- skips six letters

On the staff, an octave skips six notes, from either line to space or space to line. Both notes in an octave have the same letter name.

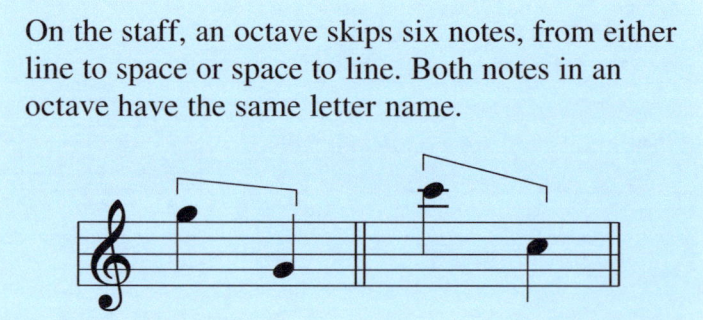

Jumping Beans

Allegro *giocoso (♩=165)

Kreader, Kern, Keveren

*Giocoso means humorous

24

COMMON TIME

C

Common Time is another name for 4/4.

Relay Race

Carl Czerny
(1791-1857)

Allegretto (♩=155)

The Primary Triads in **A Minor** are:

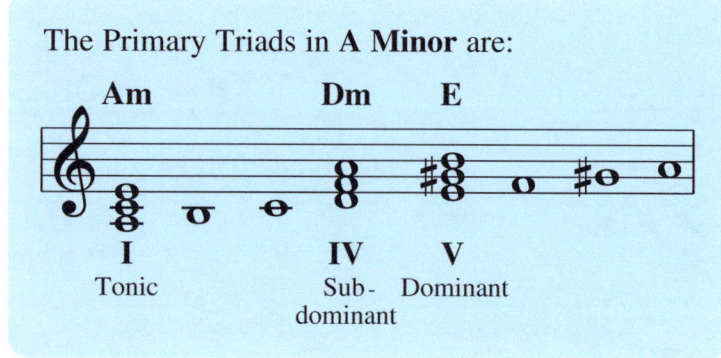

Practise these chords in **close position** before playing *A Minor Tango*:

The **E7 chord** includes D, the 7th note above E.

A Minor Tango

Phillip Keveren

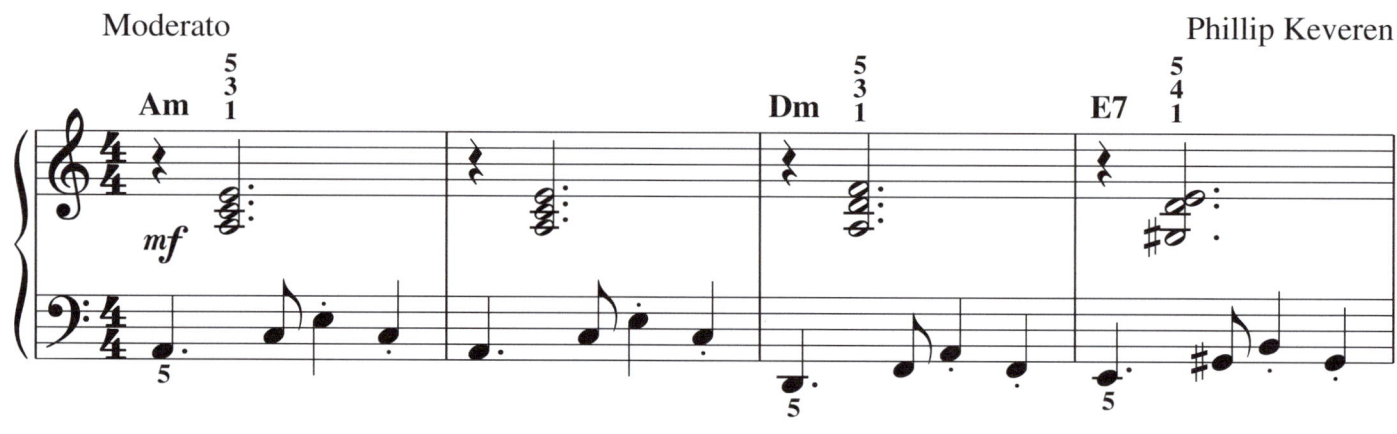

Teacher Solo

My Own Song — Improvisation using *A Minor Triads*

As your teacher plays the student part to *A Minor Tango,* improvise a new melody in the key of **A Minor**.

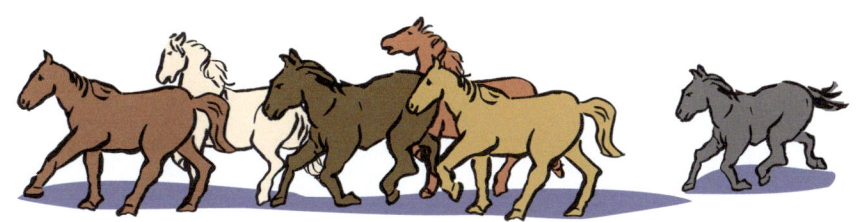

All The Pretty Little Horses

American
Arranged by Fred Kern

Slowly (♩=94)

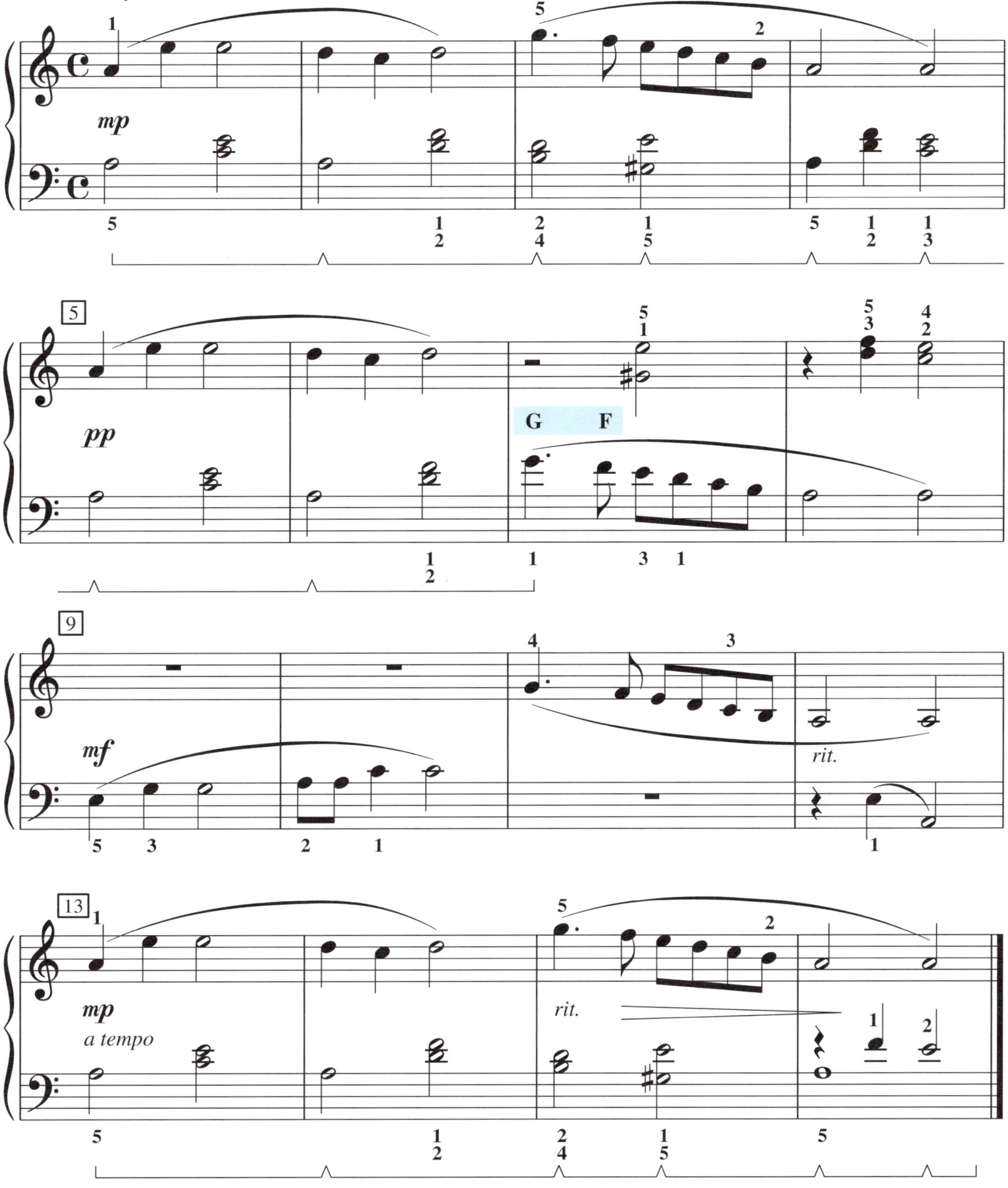

Joshua Fit The Battle Of Jericho
Theme and Variations

> **CHANGING METRES**
>
> This piece uses a different time signature for the theme and each variation:
>
> 4/4 for the Traditional style,
>
> 3/4 for the Classical style, and
>
> 4/4 for the Jazz style.

Theme: Traditional
Allegretto (♩=170)

Phillip Keveren

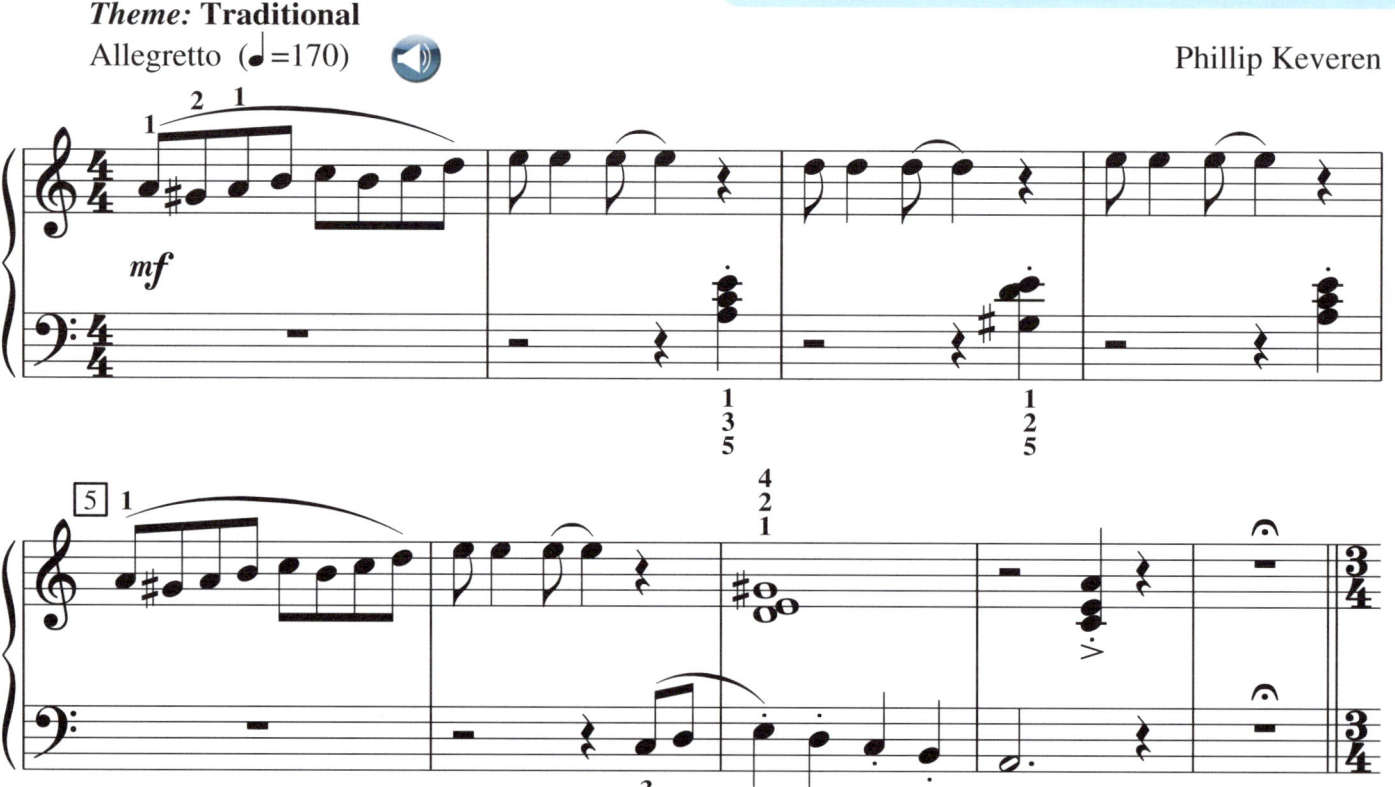

Variation I: Classical
Fleeting (♩=185) *1st time both hands 8va*

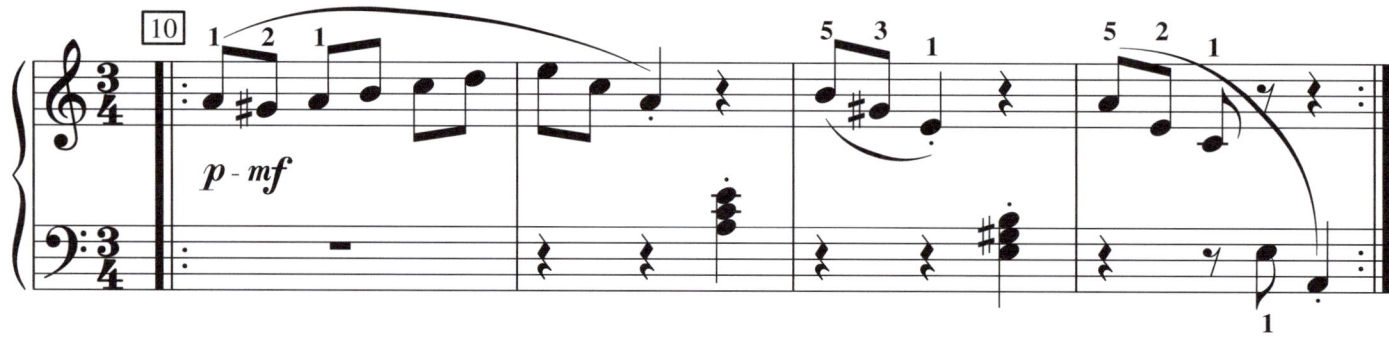

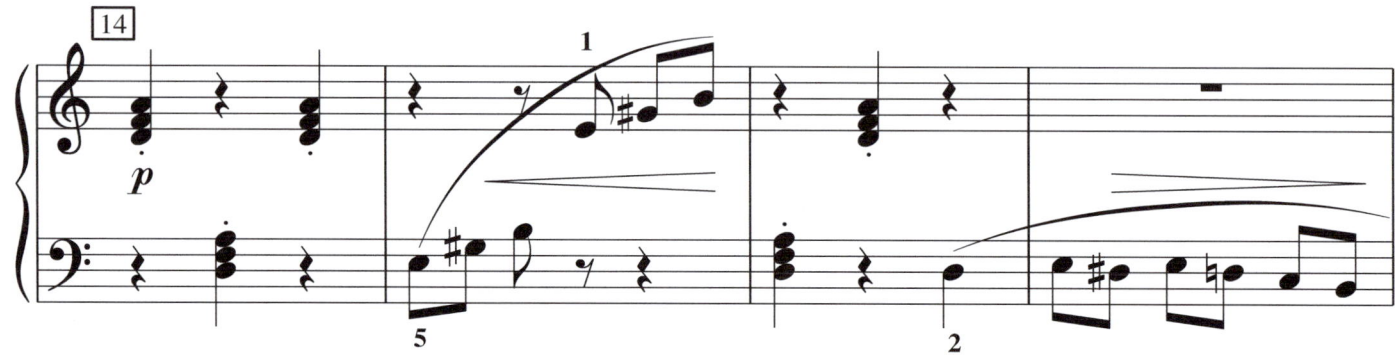

28

Variation II: **Swing Eighths**
Laid-back Jazz ($\quarternote$=150)

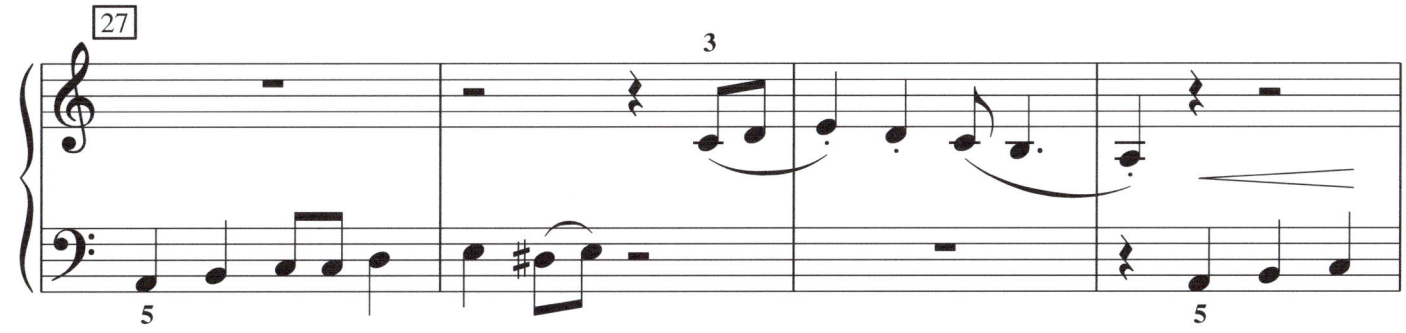

UNIT 4

G Major Scale Pattern

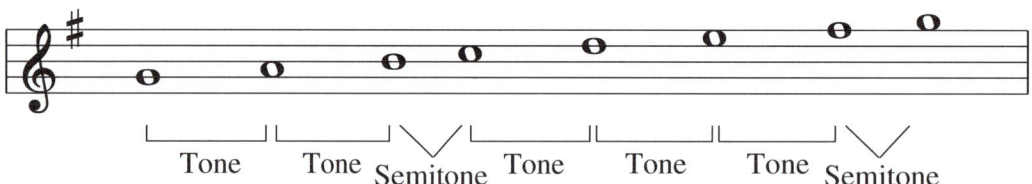

Moving On Up

Key of G Major
Key signature: *one sharp, F♯*

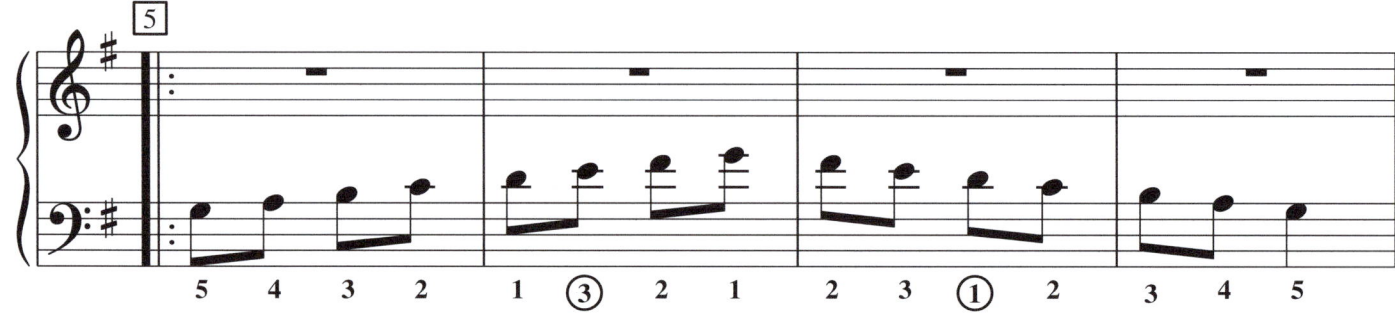

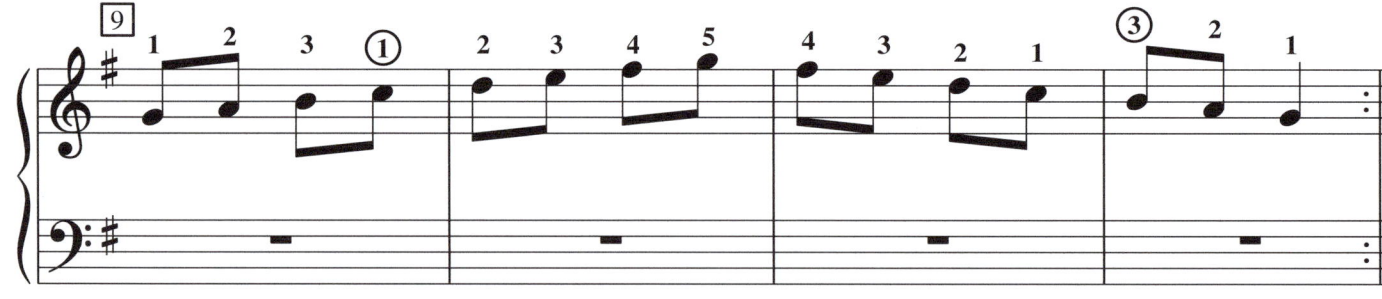

Accompaniment (Student plays one octave higher than written.)

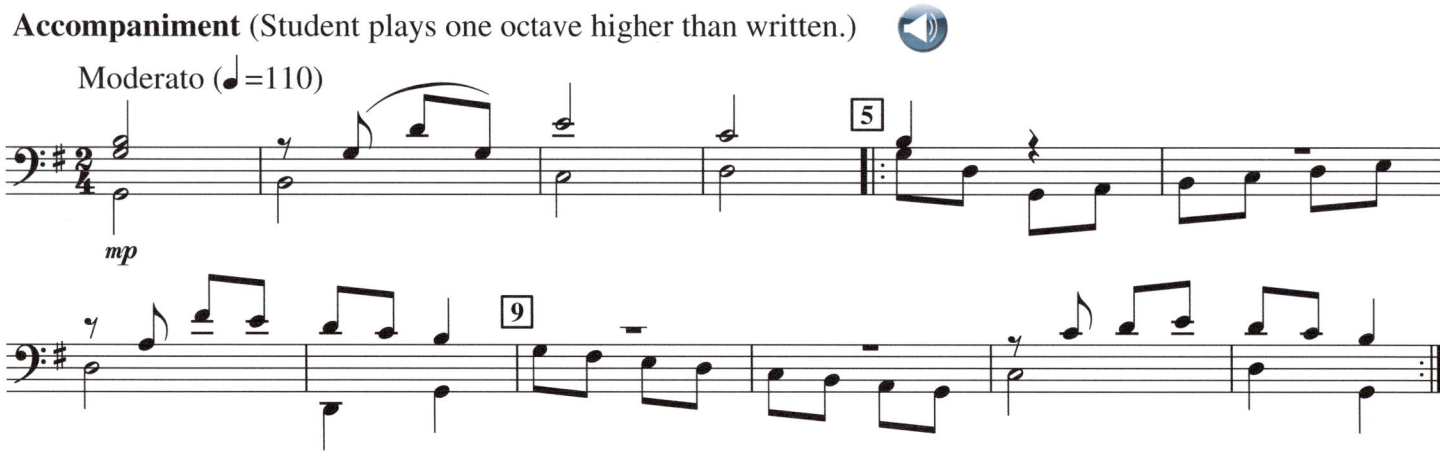

Spanish Dance

Key of G Major
Key signature: _____

Muzio Clementi
(1752-1832)
Adapted by Fred Kern

*Vivace (♩=180)

*Vivace means lively.

CUT COMMON TIME

= two beats fill the bar
= minim note gets one count

Common Time has the feeling of four beats per bar.

Cut Common Time changes the feeling to two beats per bar.

Clap and count these patterns:

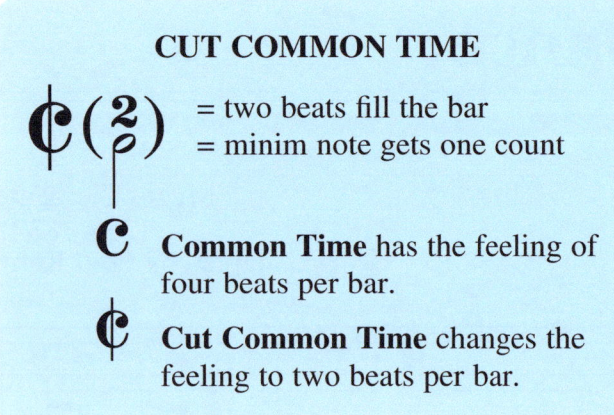

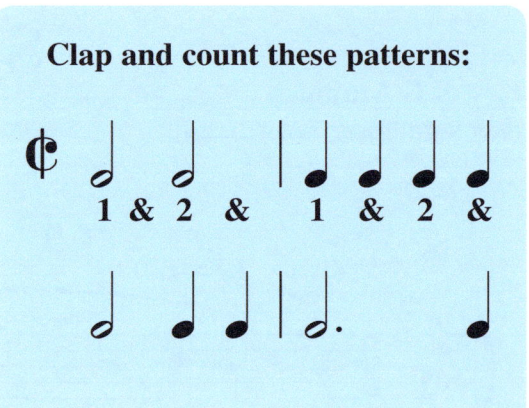

True Blues

Slowly (𝅗𝅥 =60)

Bill Boyd

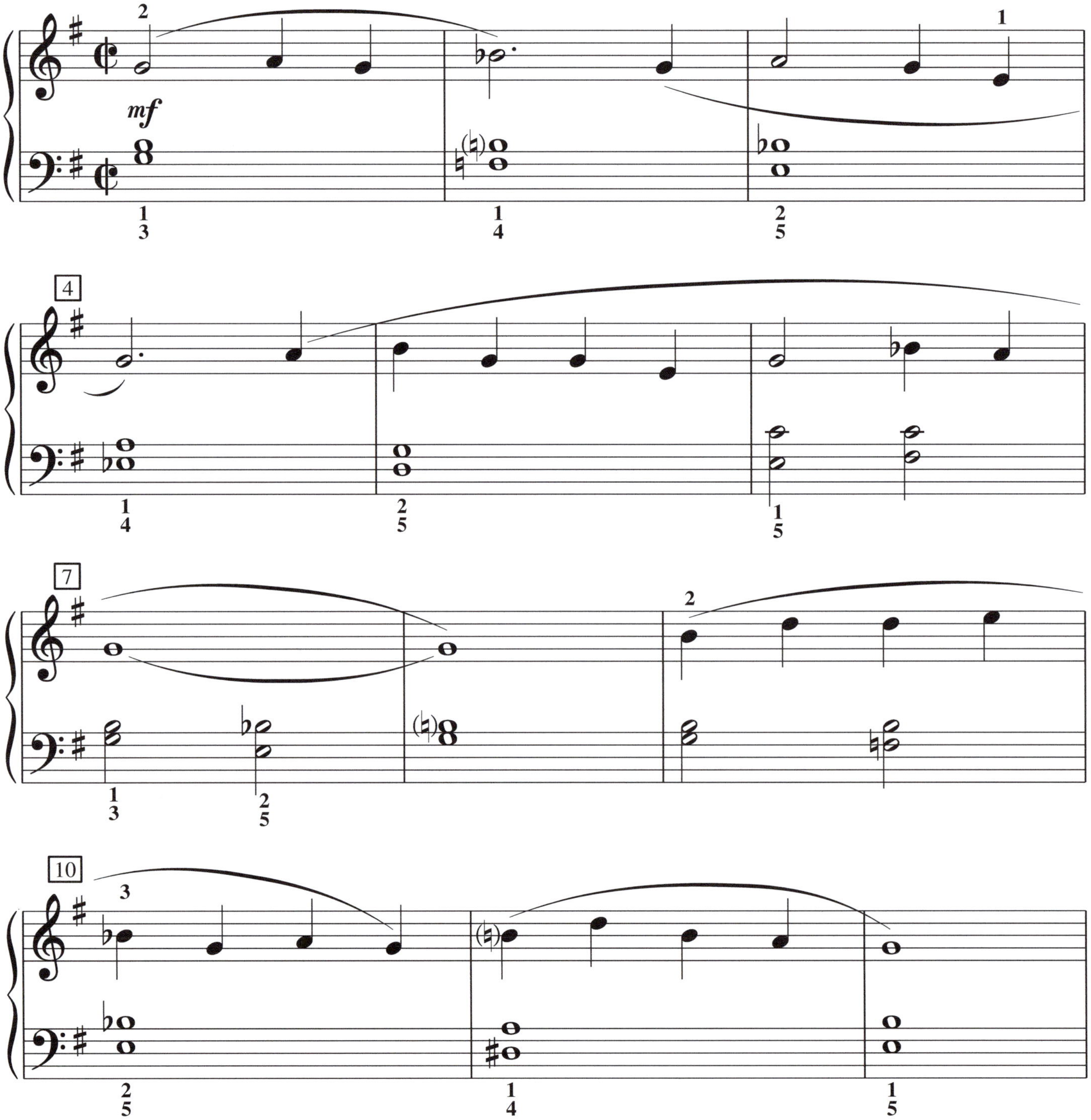

TRIPLETS

A quaver note **Triplet** fills the time of one crotchet note.

Blues For A Count

Moving along (♩=120)

Bruce Berr

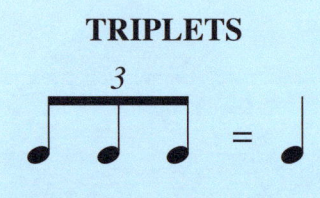

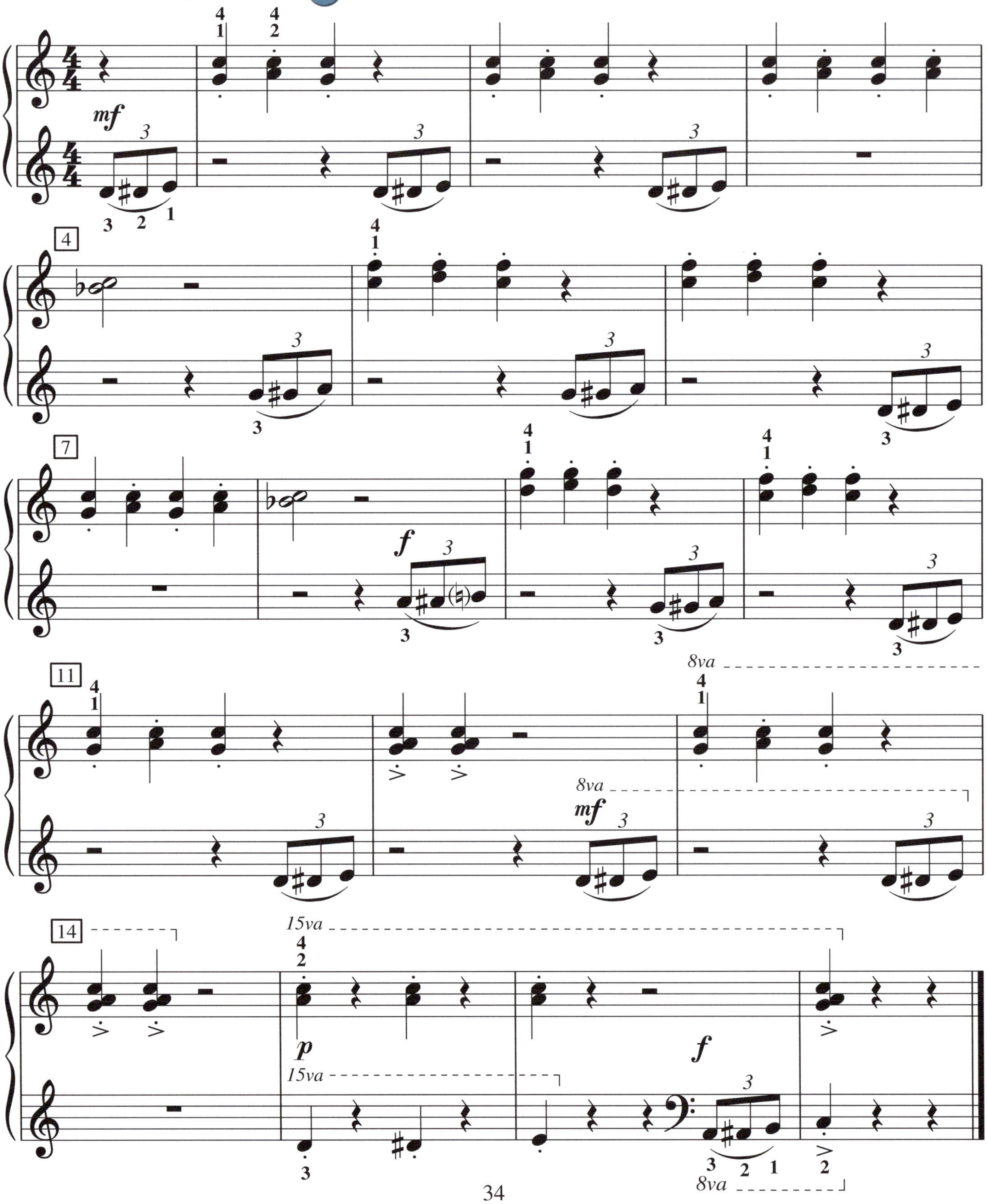

Clap and count these patterns:

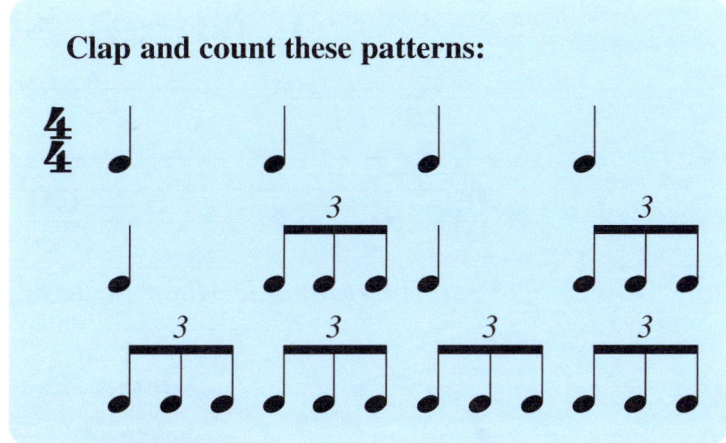

Doo Wop Ditty

Happily, in no big hurry (♩=65)

Phillip Keveren

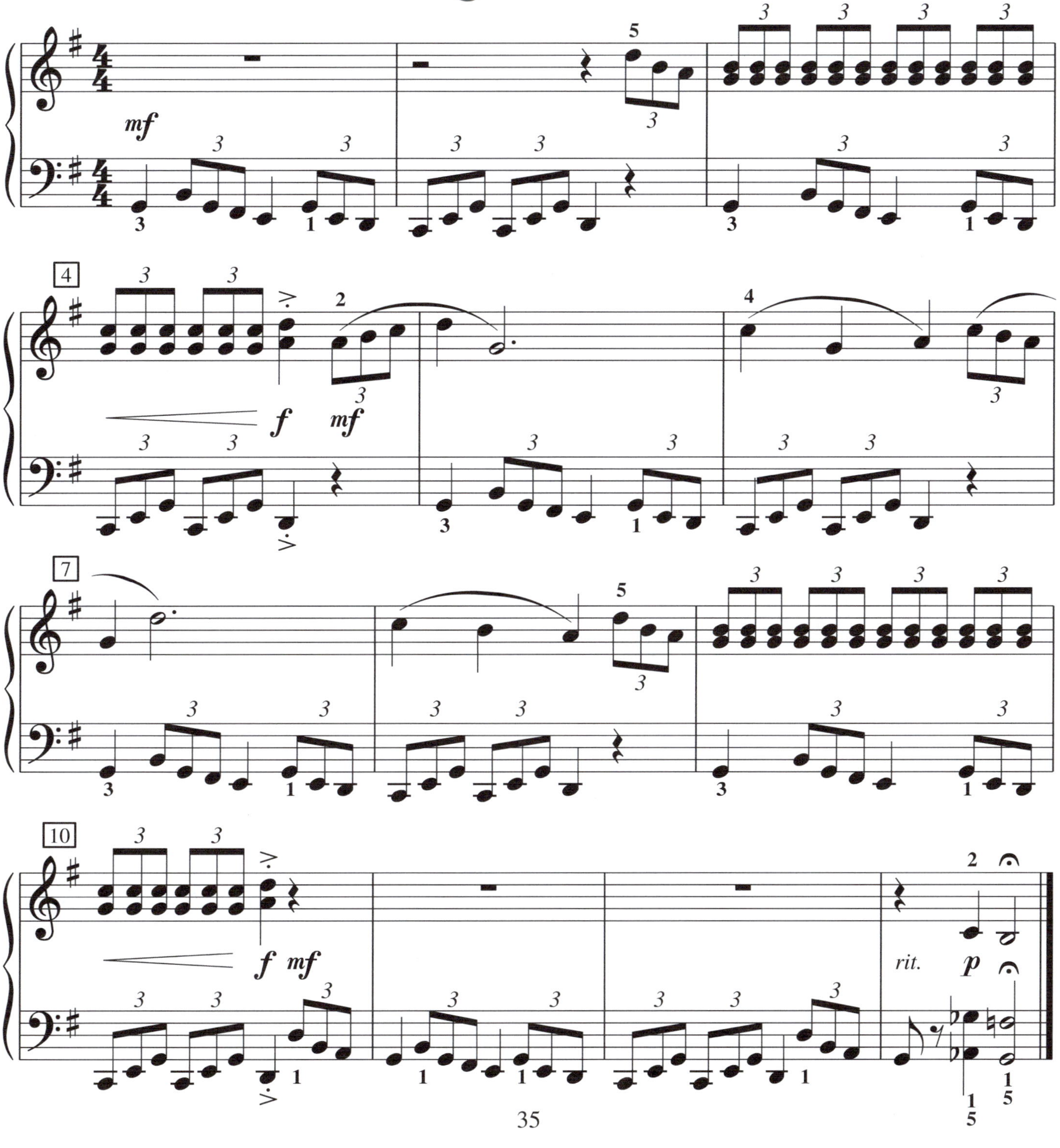

E Minor Scale Patterns
Natural Minor

The *Harmonic Minor Scale* raises the seventh note one semitone (D♯).

Moving On Up

Key of E Minor
Key signature: *one sharp, F♯*

First, play the *Natural Minor Scale* with the F♯.
On the repeat, play the *Harmonic Minor Scale* with the raised 7th (D♯).

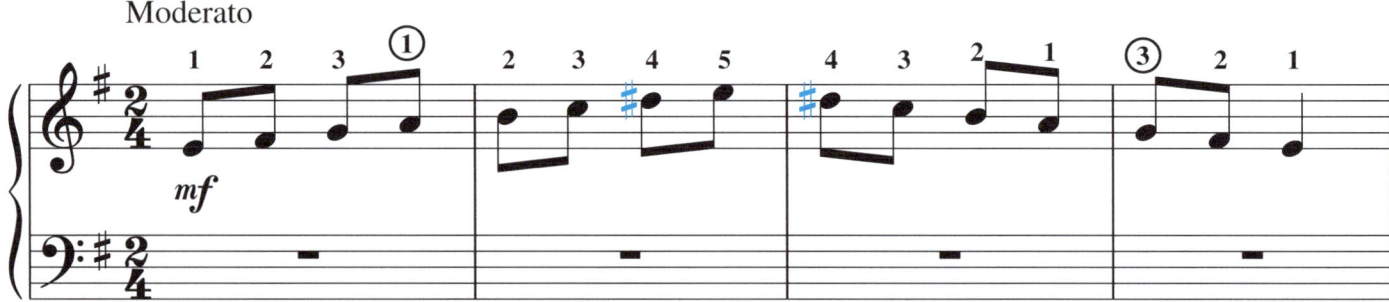

Accompaniment (Student plays one octave higher than written.)

First, play the natural form with F♯.
On the repeat, play the harmonic form with the raised 7th (D♯).

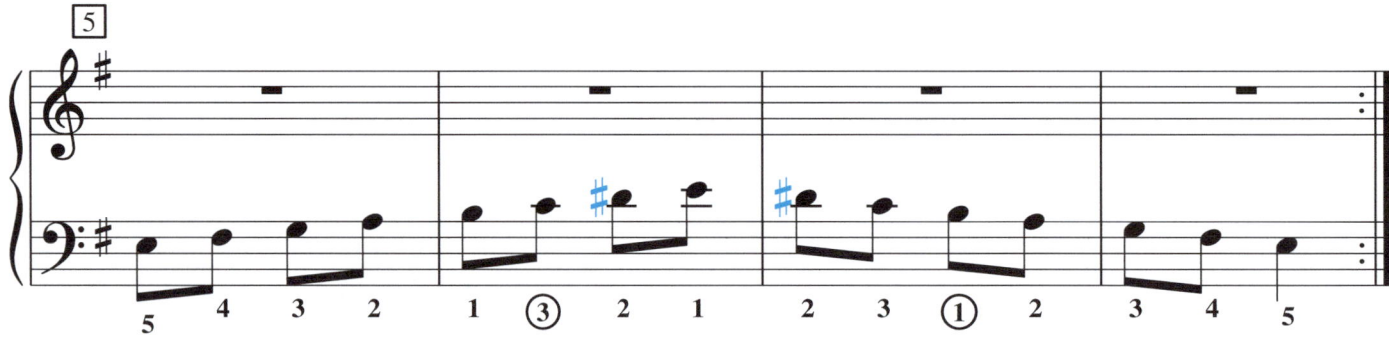

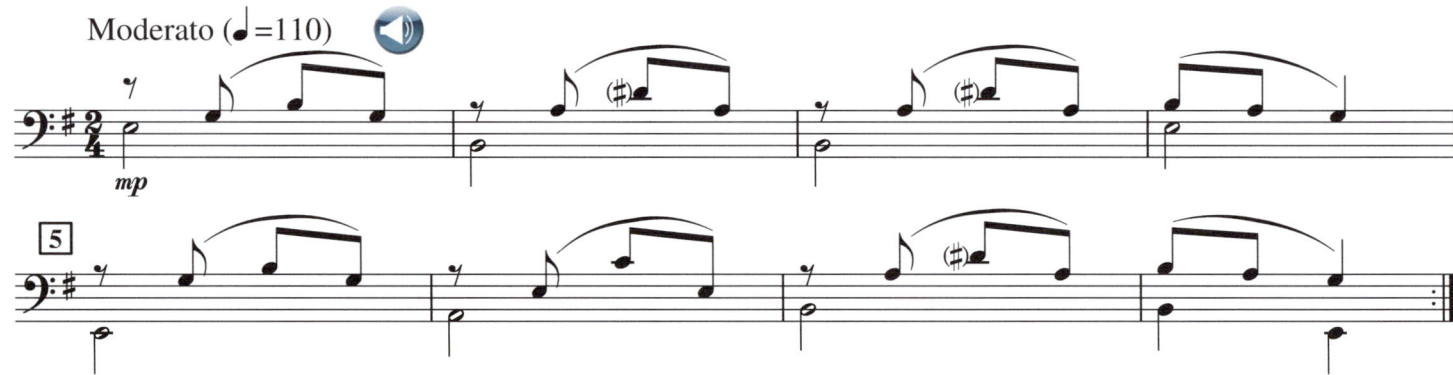

Clap and count:

Wandering

Key of E Minor
Key signature: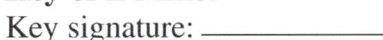

Adagio (♩=74)

Fred Kern

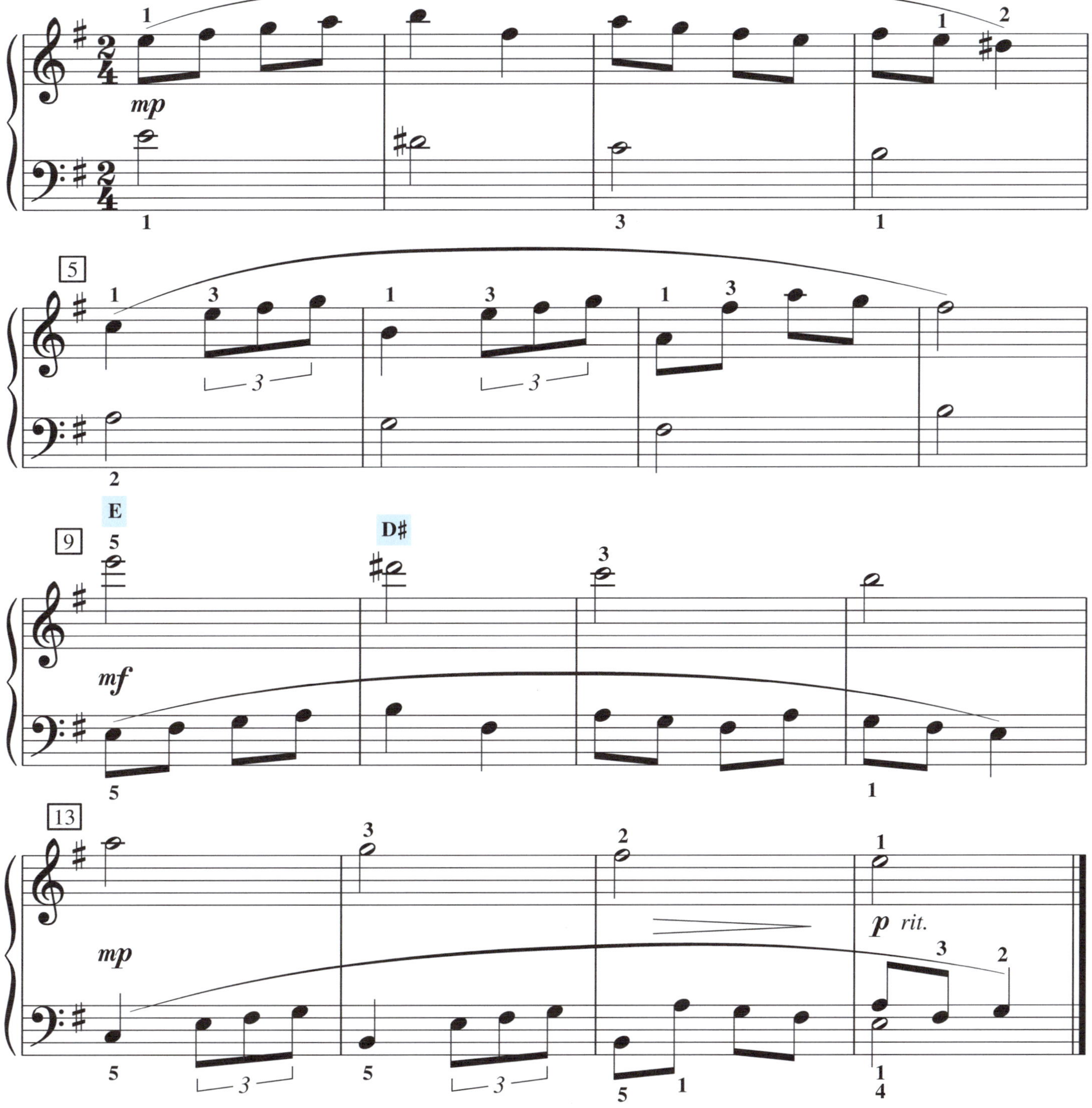

UNIT 5

The Primary Triads in **G Major** are:

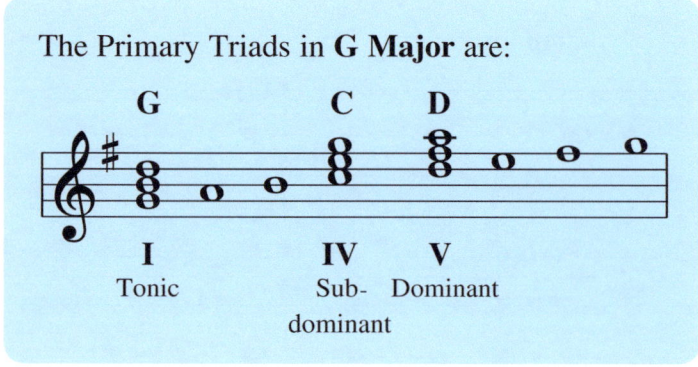

I — Tonic
IV — Sub-dominant
V — Dominant

Practise these chords in **close position** before playing *Ready To Rock*:

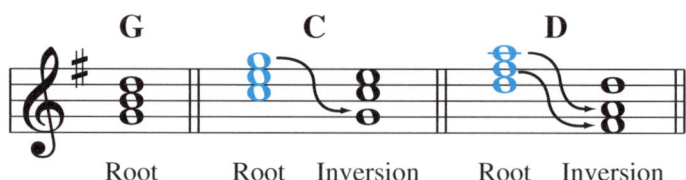

Root | Root Inversion | Root Inversion

Ready To Rock!

Rockin'

Phillip Keveren

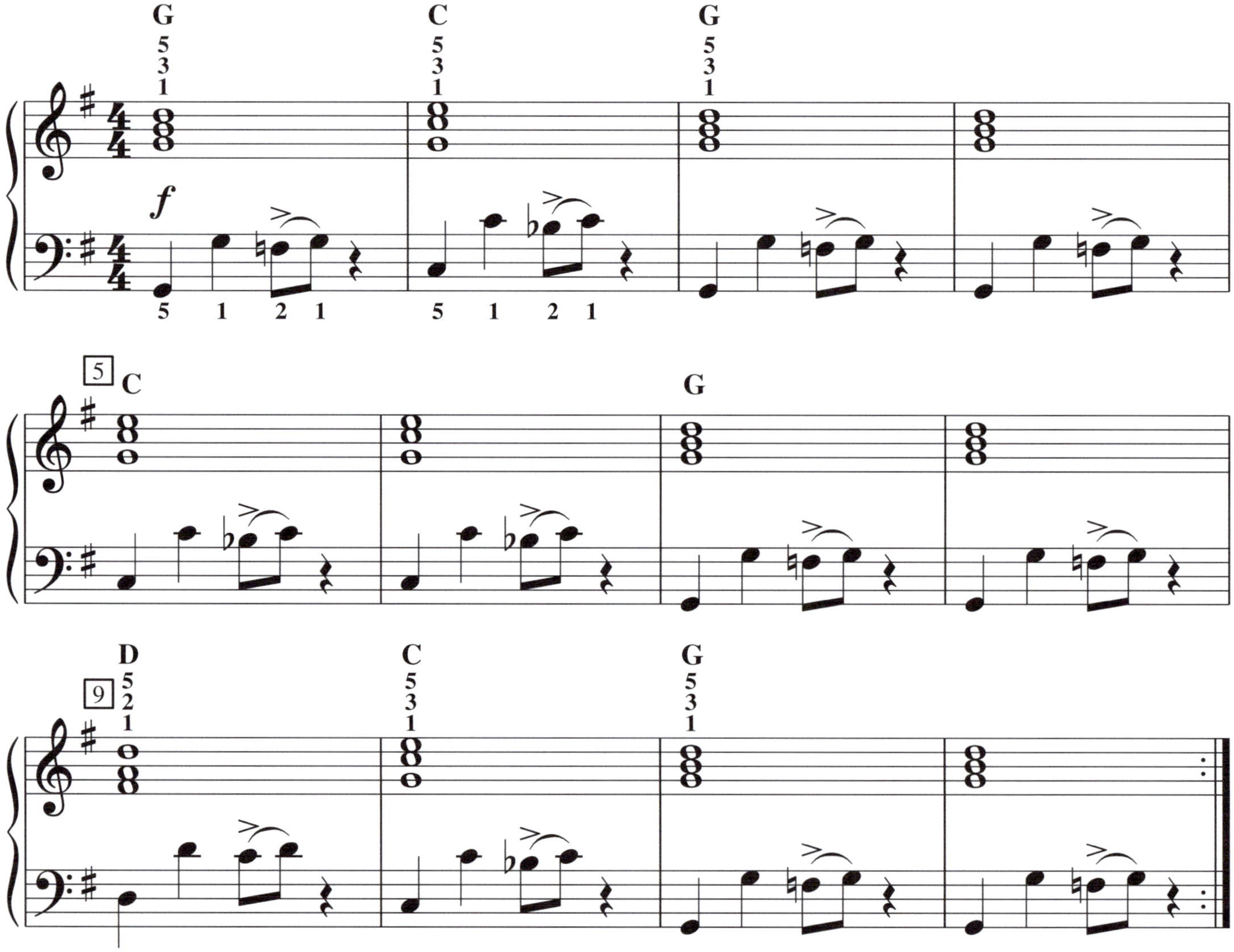

Teacher Solo (Student plays one octave lower than written.)

Rockin' (♩=120)

8va throughout

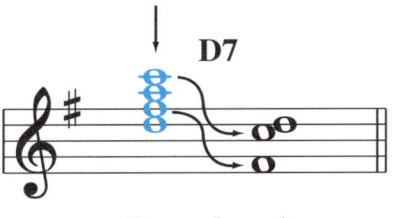

The **D7 chord** includes a C, the 7th note above D.

D7
Root
Inversion

The Bass Singer

Ludwig Schytte
(1848-1909)

Moderato (♩=100)

p
mf
5
9
13

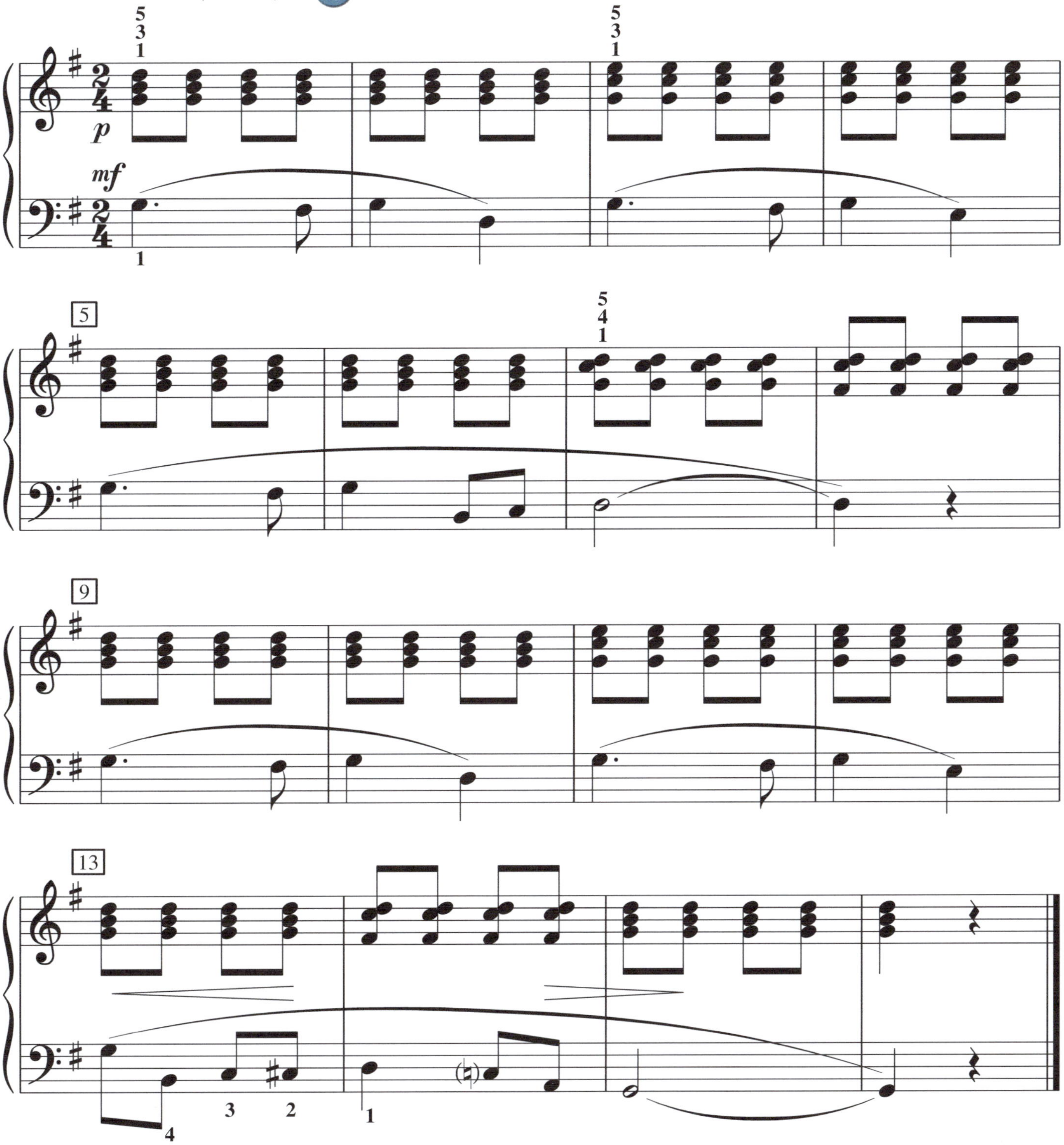

The Primary Triads in **E Minor** are:

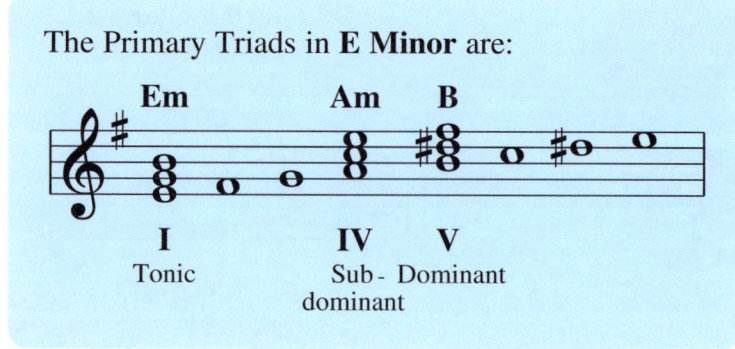

I — Tonic
IV — Sub-dominant
V — Dominant

Practise these chords in **close position** before playing *On the Prowl*:

The **B7 chord** includes an A, the 7th note above B.

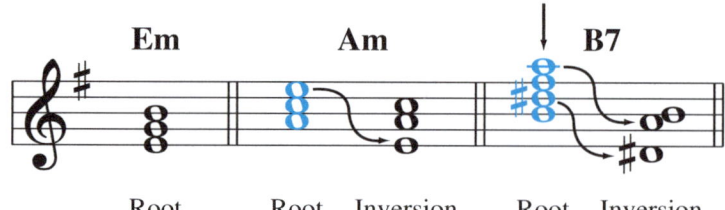

Root Root Inversion Root Inversion

On The Prowl

Phillip Keveren

Cautiously

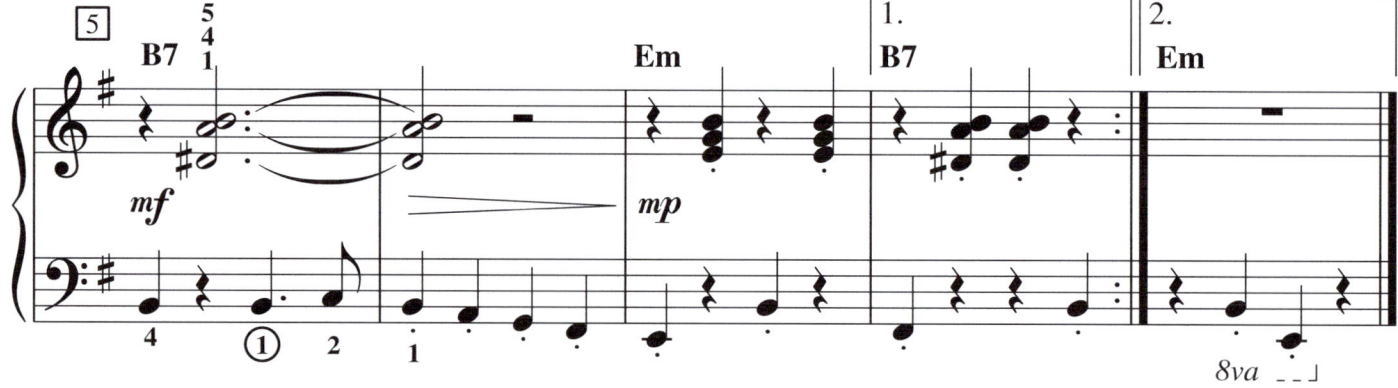

Teacher Solo

Cautiously (♩=135)
8va throughout

My Own Song Improvisation using *E Minor Triads*

As your teacher plays the student part to *On The Prowl*, improvise a new melody in the key of **E Minor**.

Starry Night

Andante (♩=98)

Italo Taranta

FINGER SUBSTITUTION

Sometimes a phrase extends beyond the range of a five-finger pattern. To keep the sound smooth and connected, substitute one finger for another on the repeated note.

41

> **TENUTO**
>
> A short line over ▔♩ or under ♩▁ a note means to play **Tenuto**. Give the note extra emphasis, holding it for its full value.

Rhapsody

Allegro (♩=180)

Jennifer Linn

Longing

Andante *con moto (♩.=35) Barbara Kreader

*Con moto means with motion.

Presto

George A. Benda
(1722-1795)
Adapted by Fred Kern

* Presto means fast.

Allegro
from *Eine Kleine Nachtmusik*

Wolfgang A. Mozart
(1756-1791)
Adapted by Fred Kern

The following information applies only to the Book/Audio package.

Instrumental Accompaniments

orchestrated by Phillip Keveren

Full orchestrated arrangements are included with this book and may be used for both practice and performance. There are two accompaniment tracks for each piece. The first is a practice tempo; it is slower and includes the piano melody. The second is the performance tempo—a little faster—and without the piano melody.

To access the accompanying audio and MIDI files, simply go to **www.halleonard.com/mylibrary** and enter the code found on page 1 of this book. This will grant you instant access to every file. You can download to your computer, tablet, or phone, or stream the audio live—and if your device has Flash, you can also use our *PLAYBACK+* multi-functional audio player to slow down or speed up the tempo, change keys, or set loop points. This feature is available exclusively from Hal Leonard and is included with the price of this book!

For technical support, please email **support@halleonard.com**

Audio Track List

	Page in Lesson Book	Track # with Solo *practice tempo*	Track # w/o Solo *performance tempo*		Page in Lesson Book	Track # with Solo *practice tempo*	Track # w/o Solo *performance tempo*
UNIT 1				**UNIT 4**			
My Own Song – C Major & A Minor	4	–	1	Moving On Up – G Major Scale	30	45	46
Rustic Dance	5	2	3	Spanish Dance	31	47	48
Carpet Ride	6	4	5	True Blues	32	49	50
My Own Song – G Major & E Minor	7	–	6	Blues For A Count	34	51	52
Mister Banjo	8	7	8	Doo Wop Ditty	35	53	54
Morning Bells	9	9	10	Moving On Up – E Minor Scales	36	55	56
Ribbons	10	11	12	Wandering	37	57	58
UNIT 2				**UNIT 5**			
Scale Preparation	11	13	14	Ready To Rock!	38	59	60
Moving On Up – C Major Scale	12	15	16	The Bass Singer	39	61	62
Calypso Cat	13	17	18	On The Prowl	40	63	64
Jig	14	19	20	Starry Night	41	66	67
Two-Four-Six-Eight	16	21	22	Rhapsody	42	68	69
Moving On Up – A Minor Scales	19	23	24	Longing	44	70	71
Allegro	20	25	26	Presto	45	72	73
Etude	21	27	28	Allegro from *Eine Kleine Nachtmusik*	46	74	75
UNIT 3							
Take It Easy	22	29	30				
Close By	23	31	32				
Jumping Beans	24	34	35				
Relay Race	25	36	37				
A Minor Tango	26	38	39				
My Own Song – A Minor Triads	26	–	40				
All The Pretty Little Horses	27	41	42				
Joshua Fit The Battle Of Jericho	28	43	44				